ACHIEVING AN
A+ MARRIAGE

52 A's And Ways To An A+ Marriage

DAVID A. EHLINE, M.DIV., MSW

Xulon
PRESS

Cindy —

I hope that you'll think this effort of mine is pretty good & that it could be helpful to couples. Maybe even be used as a source in a couples' group. With a holy hug & Christ-like love!

Dave

ACKNOWLEDGEMENTS

Sincere thanks to my sister, Judy Celis, for her encouragement and assistance in having this book published. Equally sincere thanks to Gene Plummer and Peggy Bodie for their most helpful proof- reading, suggestions, and corrections. Of course I'm most grateful to my wife, Patti, for her editing skills and support.

Preface

I once was asked what I considered to be three essentials in a successful, satisfying marriage. I answered with three words that began with the letter "A" – Acceptance, Affection, and Affirmation.

Over time I began to think of other words whose realities are essential in a fulfilling marriage: words like Apologies, Appreciation, Approval. Soon there were a dozen words that began with the letter "A" that I consider to be important, and perhaps even essential, to a successful, enduring marriage. Then I wondered if there could be 52 "A" words that might be considered the building blocks of a quality marriage. I came up with those 52 words, one for each week of the year, as good food for thought that busy couples could use as weekly discussion starters for achieving an A+ marriage. Some of the words are Actions to Accentuate, and some are Actions to Avoid. Some are nouns, some verbs, some adjectives, and some adverbs, but all require action. The order of the 52 words in each of the two categories is alphabetical, rather than in rank of importance.

Couples contemplating marriage could also use these brief thought-provokers to share openly their thoughts about the importance of each of these words in the ideal marriage. Hopefully, these "A" words will be the springboard for married couples, engaged couples, couples considering marriage, and single people who may want to be be married, to think intentionally and deeply about their expectations of marriage. From my almost 50 years as a counselor and as a pastor, I have learned that all too many enter into marriage with very little thought about their "bottom line," their "non-negotiable requirements" and their basic but absolute expectations of what they want marriage to be.

In pre-marital counseling, as well as in counseling couples whose marriage is in trouble, I routinely asked, "Why did you two decide to be married?" Invariably the answer was "Because we loved each other." But when I asked what love meant to them, or asked them to pretend that they were filming or videotaping a couple who loved each other, but who were engaged in a disagreement, how would that couple be interacting, usually there would be blank stares. "How about videotaping a couple who are showing love through actions and words of acceptance?" Again there was not much in the way of concrete and specific descriptions of how acceptance looks and sounds. And when asked, "What are your expectations of marriage?" most individuals respond with "That we love each other." But attempts to get them to expand on what that means, or what that might look like, more often than not proved to be futile.

My hope is that the thoughts in this book will be helpful to any who want not just a "C" grade marriage, but an "A+" marriage.

ACTIONS TO ACCENTUATE

Absolution
Acceptance
Accommodation
Accord
Accountability
Accolades
Admiration
Admission
Adherence
Adonai
Adventure
Advocate
Affection
Affirmation
Agape
Adjusting
Agreeability
Aid
Alacrity

Alliance
Alter
Altruism
Amends
Amiability
Amigos
Amorous
Amusement
Aphrodisiac
Appreciation
Approval
Apologies
Articulation
Assertiveness
Assurance
Asylum
Attention
Authenticity
Autonomy

<u>**ACTIONS TO AVOID**</u>

Abashing
Abuse
Acquiescence
Adultery
Advice
Aggression
Alcoholism
Apathy
Assuming
Arrogance
Archeology
Avarice
Attacking
Audacity

ACTIONS TO ACCENTUATE

ABSOLUTION

Absolution: "forgiveness"

Many people think of absolution as an act of a priest or pastor who assures the person who has confessed sins that he or she is forgiven. However, absolution/ forgiveness is essential in marriage also. Confession and apologies are crucial if a broken relationship is to be mended and healed, but absolution/forgiveness is equally essential.

What does forgiveness mean? Many people are misinformed or simply unaware of what forgiveness includes, and what forgiveness does not include. Forgiveness is not synonymous with approval. To forgive is not to approve of the offensive act or word. To forgive is not to accept as permissible the actions or words of the offender. To forgive is not to say, "Oh that's okay – hit me again!"

Many people think that to forgive is to forget. "Forgive and Forget" is such a well known cliché that we have come to think that the words "forgive" and "forget" mean the same thing. They don't. Some offenses we may be able to forget, but some we will never forget. The offense that led to a petty squabble is soon forgotten, but the adultery or the physical abuse may never be forgotten.

A preferable saying is "Forgive and Forego." To forego means to do without. To forgive is to forego the desire to get even, to forego the urge to retaliate, to forego the drive for revenge. To forgive is to forego the sense of moral superiority we inevitably feel after someone has hurt us. To forgive is to forego the rage that boils and roils within us, and that robs us of joy and peace.

We have heard and have believed that revenge is sweet. Not true! When we are filled with thoughts of revenge and feelings of rage, we hurt only ourselves. The one who caused our pain is not affected at all by our thoughts and desires to even the score. The longer we hold onto grudges, hatreds and schemes to get back at the one who cheated or betrayed or abused, the longer we will feel miserable.

However, to forgive is not something done quickly. Forgiveness takes time. Forgiveness comes after the anger, the pain, the tears, the hatred and the compulsion to strike back. And forgiveness often requires divine intervention. The saying is true that to err is human, to forgive divine.

For discussion: How do you define forgiveness? What makes forgiveness so difficult? How does an unwillingness or inability to forgive rob us of a satisfying life? The saying is "Get a life!" Why is it necessary to forgive in order to get a life? Why did Jesus teach that we should forgive an endless number of times? (Matthew 18:21-22)

Prayer: As You forgive us, help us to forgive one another.

ACCEPTANCE

Acceptance: act of accepting; state of being accepted; favorable reception

To accept: to receive a person with favor

Everyone wants to be accepted, to be received with favor. Yet from childhood on, we often feel that our acceptability is conditional. The message we get, whether given intentionally or not is "I will accept you, give you a favorable reception, if you get good grades in school; if you lose weight; if you are obedient; if you go to college; if you succeed in your career; if you marry the right person; if you come and visit us; if you give me grandchildren," and so on and so forth. Children sometimes learn in school at a very young age that they will be accepted if their drawings look just like every other student's and the teacher's drawing, or only if they excel in sports, or only if their clothing is just the same as everyone else's.

What we want is to be accepted unconditionally and fully for who we are, not for whom or what someone else thinks we ought to be. A shy person doesn't want to be coaxed or cajoled into being more outgoing. "Why don't you talk more when we go to my company's parties?; don't be such a wallflower." A wage-earner doesn't want to hear, "You're a hard worker, but you need to get a job that pays more." A wife and mother feels unaccepted when she hears, "Why can't you get back to the weight and shape you were before you got pregnant?" A husband feels unaccepted when he hears from his wife, "Why are you always in your *head* when I want to know what you *feel*?"

Acceptance means "I love you and cherish you in spite of, or maybe because of, your faults and foibles, your shortcomings and the ways you're different from me." Acceptance means "I'm not going to try to change you because I know that only you can change you." Acceptance means "You're a Republican and I'm a Democrat, but we can respect each other's points of view." Acceptance means "You're a Catholic and I'm a Protestant, but we can learn to understand and to appreciate each other's beliefs and practices." Acceptance means, "I'm a man and you're a woman, and I know that men are from Mars and women are from Venus, but we will value our differences, and not expect that I'll become a Venusian or that you will become a Martian."

Acceptance, however, does not mean that every behavior must be approved or even tolerated. Physical abuse, verbal abuse, or mental abuse should not be accepted, or even tolerated. "Hitting, slapping, kicking, name-calling, lying or cheating are not okay with me, and I will not accept those behaviors."

For discussion: How do you define acceptance? How important is acceptance to you? How do you, or how *can* you show acceptance when you and I have differences and disagreements? How do you want me to show acceptance of you? Did you feel only conditional acceptance as a child? Are there any behaviors that are absolutely unacceptable to you?

Prayer: As You accept us unconditionally, help us to accept one another unconditionally.

ACCOMMODATION

Accommodation: adaptation, adjustment, reconciliation of differences

To accommodate is to adapt, adjust, and reconcile differences. The opposite of accommodation is rigid stubbornness, and an insatiable need to be right about everything. To accommodate is to meet the other person half-way, or maybe even all the way. To be accommodating is to be willing to compromise or even to say, "You're right; I'm wrong."

But to be one who accommodates does not mean to placate. To placate is always to give in, always cave in, always be the one who is wrong. To placate continually is to ask for serious trouble. Years of placating could finally result in running away or even in murder. However, to accommodate, i.e. to be willing to give a little, to be willing to acknowledge that there's a middle ground on which both you and your partner could comfortably stand, to be ready at any time to say, "Maybe you're right" is essential in any healthy relationship.

It's a lot easier to be accommodating when you come to realize that it's silly and senseless to sweat the small stuff, and to know that most stuff is small. Discuss, debate, argue only about the things that really matter. What really matters? What really matters are values regarding the use of money; child rearing philosophies and methods; where to live; the right to one's religious beliefs and political views, etc. Some things are not open to accommodation: things like abuse, addiction, lying, cheating, dishonesty. But most areas of differences can be resolved if both individuals are willing to practice the art of accommodation.

She wants to go to an Italian restaurant, but he's in the mood for Mexican food. Accommodation needed! If nothing else, flip a coin; or play paper, scissors, rock; or draw straws. He's Episcopalian, but she's Methodist. Maybe they join a Presbyterian or a Lutheran church. He's Jewish, and she's Christian. Neither can forego their beliefs and heritage. Can they decide to honor and respect each other's religious beliefs? How will they raise their children? To accommodate one another, they will need to be creative and adaptive without forfeiting their own convictions. The keys to being accommodating are to be flexible instead of rigid, to be willing to compromise instead of insisting on one's own way, to be considerate of the other while being true to oneself, to bend without placating, to seek agreement while finding a way to meet the needs of both.

For discussion: What's the small stuff that sometimes bogs us down in spats and squabbles? How can we stop bickering over small stuff, and learn to be accommodating? What are the truly big issues that do or that could cause problems for us? How can we be accommodating on these issues?

Prayer: Give us the will, the wisdom, and the ways to be accommodating to one another.

ACCORD

Accord: to be in agreement; harmony

Accord is quite different from a cord. If accord is reached by one partner having a "cord" around the neck of the other person, and that person is coerced into agreement, that can hardly be considered accord. Accord is agreement reached without coercion, threats of "or else," manipulation, or anything other than mutual compromise and consent.

Harmony is the ideal state of marriage. In music, when two or more people sing in harmony, the blending of voices is pleasant, even though or because each is singing somewhat differently. Harmony in marriage is similar. Husband and wife need not be "singing" in exactly the same way, but their blending of voices adds to their relationship and their "song." He may "sing" baritone while she sings soprano. He may be the one who "sings" the melody, while she is "singing" alto. Neither is off key, so the result is harmony.

The way to a harmonious relationship in which the couple is in agreement requires that each person in this duet follow some basic guidelines:

- Stay "on key," i.e. stick to the subject on which agreement is being sought.

- Keep the volume such that one doesn't drown out the other; both need to be heard.

- Don't improvise, i.e. don't suddenly change the tempo of the discussion by bringing up some past grievance or some old "song" that's history.

- "Sing" with fairness. In a musical duet, it's not fair for one of the duo to try to take center stage or constantly to insist on being the star. In a marriage, both voices are equally important, and both need to be heard equally and fairly.

- In a musical duet, just as in a movie whose main characters are male and female, the audience can feel if there's chemistry between the two or not. In marriage, pretend that you're being filmed, and that the viewers will be asked to rate the degree of chemistry between the two of you.

- Do not model your discussions after those who are often seen in TV soap operas. Those characters are usually loud, accusatory, hostile, and rarely reach accord.

- When two people sing together, it's imperative that each *listen* to the other. Blending in harmony won't happen unless each is *listening* to the other. The same is true in a marriage. If accord is to be reached, both partners need to *listen attentively* to the other, and check with the other to see if they have heard accurately.

For discussion: What could we do better in our efforts to reach accord? How could we practice listening?

Prayer: Gracious God, fill us with the determination and the ability to achieve accord.

ACCOUNTABILITY

Accountability: willingness to accept responsibility for one's actions.

How many times have you heard children say, "It's not my fault; he made me do it!" or "She pushed me first!" The "innocent" one finds all kinds of reasons to put the blame elsewhere. "He started it!" "She wouldn't share!" "He called me a name!" "I didn't mean to; it was an accident!" You would think that as children mature and become adults, they would give up all childish ways, but taking full responsibility for one's actions is not easily accomplished. The tendency to blame others or circumstances lingers long into adulthood.

"I was wrong," are three very small words of only nine letters, but for some people those three little words get stuck in the voice box. Every possible excuse for one's actions come out of that voice box, but not the words that show a willingness to accept responsibility for those actions. Yet a sure sign of full maturity is the ability to be accountable, i.e. to take responsibility for one's behaviors. Maturity means many things, including giving up childish ways of blaming everyone and everything for one's own actions.

The immature adult blames his or her infidelity on the spouse! As ridiculous as it sounds, it's as if the guilty one is saying "She made me do it!" Sure she did! She put a gun to his head and told him that unless he's unfaithful to her, she would blow his head off! Or she blames her child for her abuse of that child. "Well, what do you expect? He cries all the time, throws temper tantrums, tosses his food on the floor, and writes on the

21

wall with crayons!" So that explains and justifies child abuse?! As ridiculous as that sounds, many adults never grow up, never mature when it comes to taking responsibility for their own actions. When such an immature person is married, he/she is never wrong, but consistently and easily places the blame on the spouse or the children or the boss for any domestic problems that arise. Such a person is extremely difficult to live with. It's like living with an "other-blaming" child, but much more difficult. It's more difficult because a parent can enforce punishment on a child, but not with a marriage partner. It's more difficult because often, if not usually, the spouse herself/himself is the one being blamed.

To become a mature adult may not be easy. In many ways it's a lot easier to remain a child. But no one wants to be married to a child. It is possible to grow, to mature, to become an accountable adult who takes responsibility for his or her actions. There cannot be an A+ marriage without both partners being willing to be accountable.

For discussion: What makes it difficult to be accountable? How could we help each other to take responsibility for our own actions?

Prayer: Help each of us to have the courage to become mature adults who are willing and able to be accountable.

ACCOLADES

Accolade: anything done or said as a sign of great respect; approval; words of praise

The tendency in a long-term relationship is to take one another for granted. You have your roles, and your partner has different roles. You both fulfill your roles. You're both doing what you're "supposed" to be doing. So the accolades, the words of praise, the actions that show great respect for the other cease. No need any longer to say, "That was a superb meal! Thank you for working so hard to cook good meals for us!" No need to say, "Honey, you work so long and hard for us! You have such a strong commitment to our family, both on the job and at home. Thank you!" It's not necessary to give accolades for things that are simply understood to be our responsibilities. Right? **Wrong**!

When we don't receive accolades, we may feel as if we're simply being taken for granted, and/or are simply being used. It's not that we do what we do in order to receive respect and praise. We may continue to do the expected without the signs of respect or thanks or praise. But who gets tired of those indications of appreciation and those sincere accolades? If someone says that they get tired of them and don't want them, either that person is lying or simply is unaware of his or her own needs or desires. Accolades feel good! Even if your partner acts as if he/she doesn't delight in accolades, or doesn't seem even to accept them, **give them anyway**!

My mother was as good as any mother could be. She was also a superb cook. But whenever she received a word of praise about a particular meal, she would usually find fault with something in that meal. "Oh, it was nothing," or "Well, thanks, but I overcooked the corn," or "The meringue didn't get as high as it should have." It was her way of showing humility, and her way of not becoming conceited. But she *loved* the praises she received, I'm sure! And if she didn't get them, I'll bet that she was disappointed. I learned from her that it's inappropriate and egotistic to fully accept words of praise. Then in a therapy group, the leader told me to go to each person in the group, and ask to be given a genuine accolade from each of them. My response to every person's compliment or praise was to be "Thank you; dozens would agree," or Thank you; you have very good taste!" After doing that ten or twelve times, I finally felt comfortable receiving accolades, and was able to say without embarrassment or fear that I'd become conceited, "Thank you; I appreciate that."

For discussion: Do you like to be given accolades? Do you like to give accolades? What is it about giving and receiving accolades that is easy or difficult for you? What particular accolades do you like to be given? Are there some words or actions that show respect that you don't like to give or to receive?

Prayer: Eternal Source of love, help each of us to give and receive accolades graciously and genuinely.

ADMIRATION

Admiration: sense of wonder; delight inspired by anything fine, beautiful

"Give me two reasons why you chose to marry your partner?" "That's easy – number one I respect her, and number two I admire her." And if a relationship ends, often it's because respect is no longer there, and admiration for the other has been lost.

We admire people for a variety of reasons. Perhaps you admire your spouse for his intelligence, or her sense of responsibility, or his patience, or her faith. Maybe you admire her for her work ethic, or his physical attractiveness, or her love for people, or his outlook on life. Your admiration for her may be due to her cheerful disposition, or his love of children, or the way in which she makes others feel important. But does your beloved know what you admire in him or her? When is the last time you said, "I really admire the way you listen so attentively to me and to others." Or "I want you to know that I greatly admire your generosity and your sensitivity to the needs of others." Surely there are several things that you admire in the one you love. How often do you express that admiration in words?

Many people admire famous Hollywood stars, professional athletes, wealthy entrepreneurs, and various other celebrities. But if such status and popularity are what it takes to be admired, most of us don't measure up. Consequently we may feel as if there's nothing admirable about us, and since our spouse isn't as rich or famous or handsome or beautiful as famous celebrities, we may get to the point of thinking that there's nothing very admirable about our partner either.

How sad that often we admire things like wealth and fame and status or athleticism more than we admire kindness, thoughtfulness, reliability, gentleness, and a sense of humor. When a man judges his wife's physical beauty by comparing her with the cover girl, he may not even think about telling his wife that he admires the way she shows her love for him. When she compares her husband's income with that of the millions paid to a professional athlete, she may not ever tell him that she admires how hard he works, and how diligently and responsibly he helps provide for the needs of the family.

Some people find it difficult to express words of admiration. Others may find it difficult to accept words of admiration. The only way to overcome these difficulties is to practice giving and receiving those words. It's not just a cliché; it's true that practice makes perfect. Well, maybe not perfect, but practice does make a person better at whatever is being practiced.

For discussion: Tell your beloved what you admire about him or her. Tell your partner something about yourself that you'd like him/her to admire about you. Practice sharing words of admiration with one another. Examples: "I admire your empathy for others, your patience with the kids, your honesty, your creativity." See if you can each tell the other at least three things that you admire about him or her.

Prayer: Thank you, gracious God, for the admirable characteristics and abilities that we each have. Help us to express more often and more openly our admiration for each other. Amen

ADMISSION

Admission: acknowledgement of some fault, wrong, or sin

Some people have a need to be right *always*. They simply seem to be unable to say, "I was wrong," or "I made a mistake," or "I goofed," or "I screwed up." To have to be right all the time is a sure sign of low self-esteem, lack of ego strength, and major insecurity. And to have to be right all the time is a heavy burden to bear. To mess up is human! To admit to one's faults, mistakes, and shortcomings is freeing! We've all heard the saying, "No one is perfect," but the person who can't or won't admit imperfection is, of course, fooling no one, including himself or herself. Everyone knows that they're imperfect, but some people's feelings of inferiority make it necessary for them to convince themselves and others that they're never wrong. Yet, their insistence that they are always right, and everyone else is always wrong, is in and of itself, wrong, incorrect, and destructive of relationships.

Sometimes a person who insists that he or she is always right develops a relationship with a very passive person who pacifies and placates the one who never will admit to being wrong. But over time, even the one who is always placating gets to the point of being sick and tired of forever being the one getting blamed. When the one who consistently placates has had enough, he/she will either explode in uncharacteristic violence, or will one day leave the relationship without even a note of explanation. And without a forwarding address. The person who always placates, always gives in, has even been known to resort to murder.

A sign of true maturity is the ability and the willingness to say, "I may be wrong. Let's talk." Or "I was wrong, and I'm sorry." True maturity means having the inner strength and enough self esteem to admit to being imperfect, and therefore quite capable of being wrong and doing wrong.

One partner in a relationship should not be the one who consistently admits to being the one at fault, especially if the admission is counterfeit, insincere, and simply a way of pacifying the other person. Such an admission may end the argument, but does not resolve anything. On the contrary, the one who accepts the blame when not guilty only builds up more resentment. And the one who should take responsibility for his or her actions gets off the hook without ever having to grow up. *Children* blame the other person. *Mature adults* take responsibility for their behavior.

For discussion: Why is it often difficult to admit that you may be wrong? What could each of us do to make it easier for the other person to admit that sometimes they're the one in the wrong? Could we stop making accusations, and simply say, "I would appreciate it if you would (fill in the blank) instead of (fill in the blank). Do you agree with the writer who said, "*all* have sinned . . ." (Romans 3:23)?

Prayer: Almighty Creator, help us to have the courage and maturity to admit when we are wrong. Amen

ADHERENCE

Adherence: remain devoted to; to stick fast

If you've never used any type of sooper dooper glue, you may not be aware of a couple of things about its use: first, don't get any of it on your hands because you won't be able to get it off, even with a solvent and sandpaper; and second, don't use those kind of glues if you think that at some time you'll be able to separate the pieces that you've glued together because you won't be able to do it without destroying what you've stuck together. Sooper dooper glues really stick!

In marriage there is no such thing as a sooper dooper glue to hold the marriage together. But the glue that will help the marriage endure is the absolute commitment to stick fast in the tough times just as much as in the easy times; to be totally resolved to find solutions to any and all problems, difficulties, and challenges as they arise; and to put into practice the other 51 other "A" words of this book.

Far too many people enter into marriage with the spoken or unspoken idea that if this doesn't work out, we can always get a divorce. That attitude makes it all too easy to quit. The attitude that ought to prevail is this: "I will do whatever it takes, whatever is necessary, whatever could help to make this marriage survive and thrive. I am completely committed to hanging in there and sticking fast. I will, no matter what is required, remain devoted to my spouse and to our marriage. I will seek out professional help, I will get treatment for my addiction, I will change, I will grow, I will pray, I will persevere."

That is not to say that what you do will keep the marriage intact. If your partner does not have the same commitment, and continues to be abusive, or does not overcome his or her addiction, and will not take equal responsibility for being the glue that will help to keep the marriage together, your resolve alone will not save the marriage. It takes two to tango, and it takes two to keep a marriage glued together. I have known people who have given up all of their marital expectations, including the expectation that their spouse will always be monogamously faithful, just in order to keep the marriage intact. They may do so because of religious beliefs or because they think that a dissolution of the marriage would be detrimental to the children, or because they don't think that they could make it financially on their own. But whatever the reason or reasons, they choose to remain in a loveless, unhappy, unsatisfying relationship. That is certainly commendable perseverance, but clearly not what marriage is intended to be. Adherence in a marriage is the ideal, but a sooper dooper glue-like adherence may be more harmful than helpful in some situations.

For discussion: On a scale of 1 to 10, how committed are each of us to sticking fast to our marriage? In what circumstances would you no longer be willing to adhere to the marriage?

Prayer: Lord, you stick to us no matter what. Give us that kind of commitment, but lead us to know when adherence to our marriage may not be what's best. Amen

ADONAI

Adonai: One of many Hebrew names for God

Someone has said that we are not human beings who happen to be spiritual; we are spiritual beings who happen to be human. We are spiritual beings because we ask the ultimate questions, such as "What is the meaning of life?" "What is the purpose of *my* life?" Is there one *true* religion, or do they all have some truth, or are none of them true?" "How do I decide what is right and what is wrong?" "Is there really a God?" "Is there life after death?" "Is there truth in any of the religion's Scriptures?"

In addition to asking these ultimate questions, as human beings we seem to have an innate need to be connected to something greater than what we can see and touch. On a clear night, we look up into a sky that is filled with countless stars, and we realize that we are located on a planet that looks like a blue marble when photographed from outer space. And we wonder: is there life out there? What is beyond the black hole? Our finite minds cannot grasp the thought of an infinite universe or multiverse. And we wonder, and we marvel, and we ponder whether or not there is a Creator. If there is a Creator, we ask ourselves who or what that Creator is, and if there is no Creator, then we puzzle over the question of how everything came to be. And we feel so small and insignificant when we realize how tiny and finite we are in comparison with the vastness of the infinite universe or multiple universes. And we want answers and we long for a way to be connected with something beyond this life. Somehow we yearn to feel a part of the Mystery beyond the mystery of life. We sense that there is an invisible "spirit world" to which we would like to be related in an intimate and meaningful way.

We wrestle with these ultimate questions of life, and if we don't find help in organized religion, some turn elsewhere; maybe to cults, or drugs, or crystals, or astrology, or science, or agnosticism, or atheism. But all are longing for and looking for answers to the ultimate questions that we human beings ask. All are trying to make sense out of life.

A spiritual bond is important, perhaps essential, in a fulfilling marriage. That spiritual bond can take the form of church membership and regular worship. Or it could take the form of the couple sharing daily devotions and prayer. Or that spiritual bond could be respectful discussions about life's meaning and one's purpose, even if there are differences of opinions and beliefs. Whatever form a couple's spirituality takes, it is highly important to realize that taking care of one's spiritual health is as important as taking care of one's physical and mental health.

For discussion: Do you agree that we are spiritual beings? What are we doing as individuals and as a couple to take care of and nurture our spiritual well-being? What might we do better in promoting our spiritual health? How do each of us answer the ultimate questions of life?

Prayer: Adonai, the Mystery behind the mystery of life, keep nudging us to attend to our spiritual well-being. Lead us to the Truth that will free us and bond us together.

ADVENTURE

Adventure: an unusual, stirring experience, often of a romantic nature.

Marriage can become monotonous, boring, and tedious. Go to work, come home, cook and clean, help the kids with homework, mow the lawn, do the laundry, act as chauffeur, put the children to bed, go to bed exhausted, get up with too little sleep, get the kids ready, get to work again. How often have you said or heard said in response to the question "How's everything?" "Oh, same old, same old."?

What can break the monotony and boredom of predictable routine? What can bring a sense of excitement and anticipation into the marriage? How about a little bit of adventure? How about finding ways to have some unusual, stirring experiences ? It could be a weekend away from home without the children or the pets. It could be a family vacation. It could be taking an art class together at the local community center. Maybe start a walking group, or just walk as a couple several times a week. Some might find it adventurous to join or to organize a small group for study and support. Others may find adventure in going for hikes on different trails a couple times a month. Maybe learning a new hobby, either individually or as a couple would be your idea of adventure. Dance lessons could be your adventure as a twosome. Whatever would be something new, different, and a break from the everyday routine that would be interesting and stimulating for you would be a good definition of adventure.

The dictionary definition of "adventure" is "an unusual, stirring experience, often of a romantic nature."

Many couples admit that after years of marriage, the sexual side of their earlier relationship loses its excitement, and becomes a routine, somewhat boring activity of merely going through the motions without the thrill of bygone days. Often the reason is that couples don't try anything new in their love making. "Same old, same old!" If lack of knowledge or of imagination is the reason for not trying new ways of expressing love sexually, there are plenty of books and videos that reading or viewing together might be helpful, and could even lead to a spirit of adventure in the bedroom as well as in other places.

Yes, individuals within a marriage often have different ideas of what is sexually acceptable, appealing, and worthy of experimentation. Upbringing, previous sexual encounters, sexual abuse, different religious backgrounds and teachings can and frequently do lead to conflict regarding sexual practices. Differences need to be understood and accepted, but often by open discussion agreement can be reached, and adventure can begin. Patience, empathic understanding, and mutual openness without criticism of the other are absolute requirements in this area of sexual preferences and practices. Both partners need to have a spirit of adventure and excitement in exploring and experimenting with the God-given joy of sex as one way of dispelling the monotony of marriage and of the sexual side of romance. Wasn't there an old commercial that went "Try it. You'll like it."? You may not like it, but you won't know unless you try it. And if you don't like it, try something else. But whatever you do, always remember that sex between a husband and wife is meant to be enjoyable, fun, and is intended to bond two people together in committed love.

For discussion: What non-sexual activities do you think would add adventure to our marriage? What do you think about exploring and experimenting with new and adventurous ways of enhancing our sexual relationship? How do you feel about watching videos or reading books about different ways of sexual expression?

Prayer: Gracious God, thank you for our love, our marriage, our family, and for the gift and pleasure of sex. Help us to find ways of putting adventure into our marriage, so that our life together will not be overcome with boredom and monotony, but will have new ways of being adventurous and exciting.

ADVOCATE

Advocate: a person who speaks or writes in support of a cause or person

We all need advocates, i.e. people who speak in support of us. We enter into marriage with the firm conviction that our spouse will be our most loyal and constant advocate. We expect our spouse to stand up for us, to be our number one fan, to support us in our hopes and dreams and aspirations, and to shore us up when the going gets tough. We want our partner to believe in us, to speak well of us, and to defend us when we're being maligned. In A+ marriages, each partner privately and publicly is consistently an advocate for the other. Tammy Wynette has been criticized for her popular song of yesteryear, "Stand By Your Man," perhaps because it sounds as if a woman ought to stand by her man no matter what he does or says. Or maybe she's ridiculed for that song because she doesn't say that he ought also to stand by his woman.

It should go without saying that there are times when a person cannot condone the actions of his or her spouse. Abuse is one of those times. Whether it be physical, verbal, or emotional abuse, the one abused should not accept or tolerate it. In the case of abuse, the abused spouse must become an advocate for change. The abuse must not continue. Love in the case of abuse means advocating and insisting on change. "I will not stand by you or support your abusive behavior. I will support you in whatever efforts you make to get help and to stop this abuse. If you won't change, I will end this marriage. I love you, and I want our marriage to endure and to be strong and healthy, but I will not accept or tolerate abuse from you."

If abuse is not an issue, being an advocate for your partner comes naturally. When we love someone, we naturally speak in support of that person. There may be family members who, for whatever reasons, don't especially like your spouse. As you know, parents are notorious for thinking and "knowing" that no one is quite good enough for their baby. He may not make enough money, or he may not be a hunter or a fisherman like her father, or he's not of the same religious persuasion or the same political party as her family. Maybe his skin or his hair is the "wrong" color. (When a granddaughter told her grandmother that she was engaged, the grandmother said, "It's fine with me, as long as he doesn't have red hair.)! True story.

Of course it is true that love is blind, which means that when in love, we don't see the faults, weaknesses, and shortcomings of the one we love. So if family or friends point out concerns that they have about the one we love, it would be wise and sensible to look objectively at those concerns. If they point out that his teasing of you has a mean streak, or that his racism could be a serious issue, or that his pattern of putting others down could be a red flag, or that his obvious anger could endanger you, listen up. You ought not advocate for behaviors and attitudes that are contrary to your convictions.

For discussion: In what ways would you like me to be an advocate for you?

Prayer: Show us when and how to stand by and stand up for our partner, and when and how not to.

AFFECTION

Affection: tenderness; love; fondness; feelings and demonstrations of warmth

An act of affection can be anything that communicates tenderness, love, fondness, warmth. Affection can be a touch, a kiss, a hug, a word, a gift, a gentle pat, a compliment. It can be listening attentively, conveying empathy, cuddling, holding hands in public.

We are starved for affection. We are hard-wired to give and to receive affection. We long to be touched, to be hugged, to be kissed, to be heard with empathy. New born babies wither and die if they are not touched, cuddled, caressed. We never outgrow the need to be shown affection. But not everyone's ideas about affection are the same. Different cultures express affection differently. Some people are brought up in families that hug and kiss a great deal. Others are raised in homes where affection is rarely demonstrated in any kind of physical way. Some men have been taught by example that men don't hug other males, and men don't kiss their sons, and a man doesn't show affection to his wife in public. Other men are taught by example that men hug and kiss their daughters *and* their sons, and even hug and kiss other men and other women.

In some marriages in some cultures, affection is not given except sexually. Of course, showing affection is essential to love-making, but affection is needed and wanted outside of the bedroom, and is desired as something more than a sexual advance or prelude to making love. She complains, "He only touches me, kisses me, or hugs me if he wants sex. Why can't he show me some affection just to be showing me that he cherishes and treasures me?" He complains, "She pulls away every time I want to hug and kiss her. And when does she show *me* any affection except for a good-bye peck on the cheek?"

Since backgrounds of childhood are often very different, the showing of affection to one's partner and one's children may be easy for some and difficult for others. I don't recall that my father ever hugged or kissed me or told me that he loved me. I don't remember seeing my father and mother showing affection to one another. If a man's wife comes from a home in which affection was shown regularly and routinely, but he comes from a family in which demonstrations of physical affection were non-existent, their expectations about showing affection will be vastly different. But the innate need for affection will be there for both of them, so change, compromise, and growth will be required if that unquenchable need is to be met, and is to be a source of marital satisfaction.

For discussion: How was affection demonstrated in your childhood home? What kinds of affection do you want to be shown? When and where do you want to show or be shown affection? With what kinds of affection are you uncomfortable giving, and what kinds in receiving?

Prayer: Source of all affection, enable us to show affection appropriately and comfortably. Help us to find ways of showing affection that will strengthen our marriage and our family.

AFFIRMATION

Affirmation: "a positive statement"

To affirm a person is to give him/her a compliment or tell that person something that conveys approval, appreciation, or admiration. "You write very well." "I appreciate that you always remember my birthday and our anniversary." "I am so grateful that you are patient." "I love to listen to you sing." "I not only love you, but I really like you, and one of the reasons I like you is because you have such a delightful sense of humor." "I am very thankful that you're so kind to people." "I like you because of the importance you put on spiritual well-being." "You are such a gentle and tender lover." "Thank you for that delicious meal – you're a great cook!"

Some people find it very difficult to give affirmation to another. If you're one of those people, talk to your partner or a friend or a counselor about that problem. Why is it so hard to give affirmation? Is it easier to give affirmation to a co-worker or a friend than it is to give affirmation to your spouse? Or is affirmation something that you don't give to anyone? If that's the case, do you want to change? You can, but only you can change you. Start by telling your loved one just one thing that you like about him or her. Practice, practice, practice.

My mother gave affirmation easily, but I don't recall ever getting a word of affirmation from my father, although I never doubted or questioned his love for me. I've since learned that many men cannot and do not share words of affirmation with their sons especially because they think that it's not manly, and they assume that affirmation given to a son will feminize that boy. Or some fathers, and even some mothers, think that if they give a child words of affirmation, the child will become egotistic and arrogant.

We may survive without hearing words of affirmation, but we may not truly thrive because everyone has a need to be affirmed. We all need to know that we're liked. We all want to know that those closest to us not only love us, but also think that we have some very likable and positive characteristics and qualities. Even though all of us want to be affirmed, some of us find it very difficult to accept words of affirmation. When given such a compliment, some people belittle it, deny it, and refuse to fully accept it and delight in it. If you don't or won't gladly accept words of affirmation, and don't really enjoy hearing them, why do you think that is? Are you afraid that if you accept them, and maybe even delight in receiving them, you'll become conceited? Why not simply say, "Thank you!"

For discussion: Is it easy or hard for you to give affirmation? To receive affirmation? Would you be willing to give a word of affirmation each day to those in your circle of loved ones? To receive affirmation from others with a simple word of thanks?

Prayer: You created us, and You affirm us. Empower us to affirm one another, and to gladly accept the affirmations that we are given. Amen

AGAPE

Agape (a ga' pay): non-erotic love, as of God for humankind or of humankind for God or for one another.

Erotic love is crucial and essential to a healthy marriage. Sexual love unites and bonds a couple in ways that nothing else can. Erotic love is magical, ethereal, spiritual, and just plain incredible. When the emotional climate of a relationship is healthy, sexual love is the ultimate blending of two into one.

But often the emotional climate between the two is not healthy. There are unresolved issues. There is a feeling of being used. A coolness has developed between the partners. The closeness is not there. Ardor has waned. The heat is gone.

The reasons for a decline in meaningful and satisfying sexual activity are many, including busyness, no time set aside for romance, always doing the same old same old, illness, etc. But often the reason for the drop in sexual temperature and desire is because non-erotic love is missing. Good sexual love has to be preceded by good non-sexual love.

Agape is a non-erotic, non-sexual, unselfish, selfless, self-giving love that shows care, compassion, kindness, thoughtfulness, generosity, forgiveness, and self-sacrifice. Agape love is the kind of love that loves without ulterior motives, and that expects nothing in return. Agape love does not show care and thoughtfulness in order to get sex or something else as his or her pay-off.

Agape love is the love that God has for people. It's unconditional. It has no strings attached. No matter what we do or don't do we can't get God to stop loving us. A marriage needs agape love as its foundation, as its cornerstone, and as its ongoing principle. In healthy, strong marriages, each person loves the other unconditionally, and each gives themselves totally, even sacrificially to the other.

To see agape love in action, go visit a nursing home at meal time. There you will see an older couple sitting across the table from each other. One is the resident of the care center, and the other is the non-resident spouse who comes every day to feed his or her beloved, to read to her/him, and to take him/her for a walk in her/his wheelchair. He comes every day, even though he's aware that she may not know who he is. That's agape love. A self-giving, selfless, expecting nothing in return kind of love. You can also see that kind of love in a parent who cares tenderly for a multi-challenged child.

For Discussion: What are some ways in which we show an agape type of love in our relationship? Why is such love important?

Prayer: Thank you for your unconditional love. Fill us with your Spirit that we will be able to show agape love to one another. Amen

AGING, ADJUSTING, AND ADAPTING

Aging: growing older or maturing. Adjusting: altering or changing to fit circumstances. Adapting: changing to conform to new conditions.

The old saying is that if you can't learn to bend, you'll break. That saying is especially true in marriage. If you can't bend, adapt, and adjust, the marriage will break. Change is inevitable when it comes to getting older, as well as when it comes to marriage. Years ago, someone said that if a marriage is to last, the couple will need to remarry seven times: after two years, after the first child, after forgiveness, after the children leave home, after menopause, after retirement, and after moving to a care center.

As we get older, circumstances change, expectations change, responsibilities change, hormones change, hopes and dreams change, interests change, bodies change, physical appearances change, memory changes, stamina changes. Individuals in a marriage must adjust to these and other changes, or else!

In some ways we always remain the same person, but as we age, and as circumstances, situations, responsibilities, and physiologies change, we become different from the person we were at age 18 or 22 or 35 or 50. A shy and reserved woman at age 20 may become more outspoken. A man who was not interested in church or religion at age 30 may become very active in church. A man, who as a teenager was not attractive to girls, may at age 35 or 40 become very appealing to women. A stay-at-home mom becomes a career woman, and the 25 year old handsome groom becomes overweight and wrinkled.

One of the most challenging changes to adjust to is menopause. After menopause, sexual interest may decline significantly, especially if the woman has health-threatening reactions to hormonal therapy. Even with the intake of hormones, a post-menopausal woman will experience thinning of vaginal linings and diminishment of natural lubrication, resulting in uncomfortable or even painful intercourse, which can result in a reduction or even disappearance of sexual desire. Men also experience a change in their sex drive. At age 40 or 50 or 60, his desire for sexual activity may decrease significantly. Erectile dysfunction is common among aging males. The sales of much-advertised remedies for E.D. are proof of that! In some marriages, these drugs bring a welcome return to a satisfying sex life. However, these drugs have also been dubbed "The Divorce Drugs," because with them the husband may want to have frequent intercourse, whereas his post-menopausal wife wants little or nothing to do with sex, and ultimately one or the other files for divorce over the issue.

Dementia, loss of stamina, hearing and visual impairments, mobility issues, reduced income, inability to care for the house and yard, difficulty in adjusting to the empty nest and/or retirement — all require adjusting and adapting if the marriage is to remain healthy. Be prepared!

For discussion: What changes have we experienced already? What changes might we expect? How can we prepare to adjust and adapt to inevitable future changes?

Prayer: As we change, and as circumstances change, help us to adjust and adapt successfully. Amen

AGREEABILITY

Agreeability: ready to consent

Some couples argue and hassle over just about any-thing and everything. Their relationship seems to be based on conflict, and the glue that holds that relation-ship together is debate and disagreeability. If that's you, and that works for you, so be it! But most cou-ples find that chronic conflict causes their relationship to crumble. Ongoing disagreements between spouses about almost every issue that arises is not usually a marriage-enriching thing. The opposite is usually the case. Disagreeability divides.

To be agreeable means being ready to consent. To be agreeable means to have a mindset and an attitude of "I don't have to be right all the time; I don't have to get my own way every time. It's not only right but a good and positive characteristic to be agreeable." But agreeability does not mean to be nothing but a doormat or a nonen-tity who has no opinions, or a nobody who always com-plies with his or her partner. Agreeability means being ready to consent, but doesn't mean consenting with the position of the other person. Agreeability means being ready to consent that the person with whom you dis-agree has the right to his or her opinion, just as you have the right to your opinion.

In most marriages there are subjects and issues on which the couple always have and probably always will disagree. She's a Democrat and he's a Republican. He loves golf, but she thinks it's a silly game. She likes love stories, and he likes action thrillers. She supports animal rights causes, and he's a hunter. In those kinds of situations it's best simply to agree to disagree, but without ongoing rancor, or a conviction that you have a divine and moral obligation to change the mind of your spouse. Just let it be. Or better yet, grow into being understanding and respectful of the other's opinion and point of view without thinking that you have to give up your convictions. Of course, if he says that it's okay for him to beat his wife and kids, and he refuses to change that conviction, the wife must not allow herself or the children to remain in that situation.

Unless you're both the kind of people for whom argumentation and an aura of disagreeability are turn-ons, explore together ways of giving up those often unpleasant spats that sometimes escalate into destructive and divisive fights. What's behind this apparent need to change the other, and to be the one who's right and needs to prove that the other is wrong? What's the big deal? Opposites attract so turn your differences into attractions. How can you learn to love your spouse even more, *not in spite of* his or her differences and disagreements with you, but *because* of them?

For discussion: Talk about the questions raised in the above paragraph. Do so as you practice a posture of agreeability, i.e. a readiness to consent.

Prayer: Thank You that we're not the same in all things. Thank You that each of us is an independent thinker. May we have the strength and maturity to respect each other's opinions, even though we may not agree with those opinions. Bless us with a spirit of agreeability. Amen

AID

Aid: help, assist

While I was growing up, gender roles were clear and clearly understood. The man went to work, and the woman was the homemaker. *He* cut the lawn, washed the car, put on the storm windows, and raked the leaves. *She* did the cooking, the cleaning, the laundry, and the raising of the children. Those roles were exclusive, and the lines of roles were rarely crossed. She never cut the lawn or raked the leaves, and went to work outside the home only in an emergency. He didn't know how to boil water or clean a toilet or wash clothes or talk to the children. She didn't help him with his roles, and he didn't assist her with her roles.

Times have changed, and role definitions have changed. Yet the woman still assumes the major responsibility for cooking, cleaning, laundry, and child-rearing, even though she has a full-time job outside of the home, and works at that job as many hours as he does at his. In many households, it's quite acceptable for her to cut the lawn and wash the car, but not that acceptable for him to cook meals (except if the meal is grilled on the deck or the patio!), or to change diapers or do the laundry. Some would say that the biblical story of creation in the book of Genesis indicates that God created man first, and then created woman as his help-mate. Therefore it's okay for the woman to help the man, but not okay for the man to help the woman! What a convenient rationalization and justification for him! But a gross misinterpretation of Scripture. The Bible makes it perfectly clear that marriage is to be a relationship of equals, and that each is to love the other totally. Among other things, to love is to aid, assist, help the other in whatever way he or she needs aid.

In some homes, whoever does the cooking is relieved of cleaning up after the meal, and the one who didn't cook is the one who clears the table and counters, and does the dishes. In other families, she may do the laundry, but he folds and puts the clean clothes in their proper places. Some couples take turns in getting up during the night when the baby cries. He calls for a baby sitter as often as she does. Maybe it's one of his responsibilities to do the vacuuming, and she does the dusting. If he gets off work before she does, he picks up the children at the day care center or at the home of the child-care provider. Perhaps they alternate when it comes to buying groceries while the partner stays home with the children. Together they go to parent-teacher conferences. In some families the woman manages the finances, while in others that's the responsibility of the man. In other families, she is more of a handy-Mandy than he is a handy-Andy. Both may bring home a paycheck, and both believe that marriage is a partnership in which *mutual* aid, assistance, and help are given freely.

For discussion: How would you like me to help you more than I do? What do you think of role responsibilities that are determined by gender alone? Do you think that there are some chores that a woman simply cannot and should not do, and some that a man can't and ought not do?

Prayer: God, our *Help,* aid and assist us in making our marriage a true partnership of aiding one another.

ALACRITY

Alacrity: promptness

All too often, couples put off, delay, procrastinate, and avoid discussing issues that have come between them. By the time they get around to talking about the silence that has pervaded their relationship, they can't remember what they were arguing or fighting about! So they make up without resolving anything.

To have an A+ marriage, it is essential to deal promptly with issues on which there has been disagreement. Far too many couples live by the old saw "Why do today what you can put off until tomorrow?" The answers to that question are many: don't delay because you've lost a day or days that you could have been close to each other and enjoyed; don't delay because by the time you get around to talking about the problem, you may have forgotten what the problem was; don't delay because even though you may have forgotten the issue, the issue has not left your mind/psyche; be prompt in resolving divisive issues because the sooner you get the problem resolved, the sooner you'll be in tune, in touch, and in love.

That is not to say that you should deal with troublesome issues in the heat of anger. Anger tends to shut down our rational brain, our ability to reason, our empathy, our ability to understand the other, and our capacity to compromise. But don't say that you need a day or two or a week or two to regain your anger-free sanity. Talk through the problem to some kind of resolution before you end up sleeping in two different rooms.

Alacrity, or promptness, is key to problem resolution. If your tendency is to wait, delay, procrastinate, you run the risk of never getting around to dealing creatively and rationally with the issue that caused the rift between the two of you. Then that issue is buried and goes underground. After enough of those burials, that issue explodes in a gigantic volcanic eruption when triggered by that same or a similar disagreement. Such explosions can and do result in serious catastrophes, including physical or verbal abuse, abandoning the other without explanation, domestic violence that can end with police intervention, and an ugly divorce.

Don't delay! Talk today! Get down to the nitty-gritty before things get beyond repair!

For Discussion: What prevents us from dealing promptly and constructively with problems as they arise? What could we do so that we addressed differences within a maximum of 24 hours? Are there things that I could change that would make it easier for you to discuss issues with me? Why do you think that it's risky, and maybe dangerous, for us to delay discussions about things on which we disagree?

Prayer: Gracious God, help us to talk openly and constructively about our problems in a timely way, and enable us to resolve differences as they arise, rather than procrastinating about them. Help us to speak and listen to one another in ways that show respect for one another, and that will lead to solutions.

ALLIANCE

Alliance: a close association for a common objective

Obviously every marriage should be a close association, but what ought to be the common objective of this close association? The objective varies from couple to couple. For some the objective is to have children. For others the objective is to have fun. Although infrequent in recent times, for some the objective is to make sexual love-making religiously moral. During the course of my career as a counselor and minister, the answers to my question of "what is the objective of your marriage?", answers ran the gamut, but the most frequent answer was, "What do you mean? We've never talked about an objective. We just want to be together because we love each other."

What is the objective of your marriage? Why be married? One response might be, "We just want to love and be loved." Hopefully, that's the goal of each married couple. Beyond that is there a more specific objective for this your close association that is called marriage? "We want to have a family." Okay, but what if you don't have children? And what is the objective of your marriage after the children have grown up and have left the home? What will be your objective as empty nesters?

Nations form alliances for many reasons: defense, trade, cultural exchanges, scientific exploration and advancement, etc. Neighbors form alliances for protection, child care, homeowners associations, neighborhood improvements, political campaigns, etc. Churches form alliances with other churches in order to provide joint educational opportunities, to share building space, to sponsor ecumenical community-wide worship services, to join forces to meet community needs, etc. Ethnic groups form alliances for mutual support, for helping one another, and for retaining the culture and practices of their particular ethnic group.

What might be some possible objectives for your marriage? One objective might be to encourage and help enable each of you to reach more and more of your potential. If she wants to go back to school to finish her degree, will he object and protest? If he wants to get more involved in his spiritual growth and development, will she cooperate or accuse him of becoming a religious fanatic?

Another objective might be to work together as a team to focus on a common commitment to promote social justice or to work together on another cause that is near and dear to each. For some, the objective of their marital alliance could be to make a lot of money in order to give away a lot of money. Others might have the objective of fostering or adopting special needs children, or children who have been abandoned in other countries, or older children for whom placement is difficult. Other couples may have as their objective that of working together as a team in a church or in a faith-based organization that serves youth.

For discussion: What are the objectives of our marriage?

Prayer: Help us to accomplish in our marriage some worthy objectives that we might not be able to accomplish as singles.

ALTER

Alter: to change

Most people have some difficulty with change. We seem to like things the way they are. Change is unnerving and upsetting to many of us.

It's especially challenging and difficult to change ourselves. Sometimes, however, we must make changes if our relationship is to survive and thrive. For example if a person has a tendency to lose his or her temper and become physically or verbally abusive, change is not only called for, but is imperative. If a parent is negligent, change is not an option, but an absolute necessity. If a person spends money that he or she doesn't have, and finds himself in chronic debt, it is certain that unless change occurs, disaster will soon happen.

These examples are the extreme, but other kinds of undesirable behaviors also may require a person to change. What if you're a person who is always late, and your spouse is a person who is always on time? And what if this difference causes arguments and dissension in the relationship? Someone is going to have to alter their ways. What if he doesn't help with any domestic chores, and she expects some help from him? Or what if she is a nagger and fault-finder, and he says that he's had enough of criticisms and put-downs? Change is going to have to occur, or else!

What are the necessary steps if change is to happen?

- A willingness and desire to change

- A commitment to change

- A systematic and consistent effort to change

- A refusal simply "to try" to change, because 'trying' is usually just an escape hatch to excuse oneself when change doesn't happen

- A partner who is patient and who gives positive reinforcement when the change is evident

- Sometimes counseling and/or medical intervention is necessary

- Divine guidance and empowerment, and a willingness to ask for and accept God's help

- Hard work and a willingness to accept full responsibility for one's behaviors

- No game playing such as "What can you expect from someone who had such rotten parents?" or "Poor me, I have an impulse control problem," or "I am the way I am, so you can take me or leave me," or "The way I am is God's fault or the fault of the war I was in or the fault of the fact that my father abandoned me."

Change is never easy. But change is possible. With God all things are possible. With total dedication and commitment to change, and with the help of God and others, anyone can change.

For discussion: What changes do we each need to make?

Prayer: God, help us to make the changes we need to make in ourselves. Amen

ALTRUISM

Altruism: unselfish devotion to the interests and welfare of others

One of the problems with the English language is that we use the word "love" in so many different ways. We say "I love you," and we say "I love chocolate," and "I love that song," and "I love this dress," and "I love my cat," and "I love to dance." Yet the word "love" in each of those sentences means something different. What do you mean when you tell your spouse that you love him or her?

Some people are so in love with the idea of love and of being loved that just hearing those three words "I love you," is enough. But it really isn't enough. Everyone has a longing to know that those words mean something specific, something special, something unique. We want to know that when we're told "I love you," it means that we're the one above all others. We want to know that the one who says those words means that he/she cares for no one else as much, cherishes no one else as much, treasures no one else as much. And whether we acknowledge it or not, when those words are spoken to us, we want them to mean, "I will give unselfish devotion to you, your interests, and to your well-being." What we really want is altruism. What we desire is that the one who loves us, will love with altruism.

A woman came to me for counseling, complaining that her husband beat her up on a regular basis. He'd get drunk, come home, pick a fight with her, and then slap her, hit her, push her, and bruise her. She said that she wanted a divorce. I asked her to bring her husband with her for an appointment the following week. When he came in with her, he immediately began to cry, saying that he loved his wife, and didn't want a divorce. My response was "Beating her up is sure a strange way of showing love." Name-calling, spending money recklessly, unwanted teasing, mean-spirited criticism are also strange ways of showing love. They do not show unselfish devotion. They do not demonstrate love.

It's not enough simply to say "I love you." Love is not just words, and love is not just a feeling. Love is to be translated into actions. To truly love another is to have unselfish devotion to the interests and well-being of that person. To love another is to practice altruism. To practice altruism is to treat the loved one unselfishly, seriously taking into consideration their interests and needs. Altruism does not abuse, is not selfish, and does not insist on having its own way. I've seen all too many people who treat their cat or dog with more altruistic love than they show their spouse.

For discussion: For a good description of altruism read chapter 13 of first Corinthians in the New Testament. How would you explain altruism to an 8 year old? How do you want altruism to be shown to you?

Prayer: Gracious God of altruistic love, give us Your spirit of altruism to one another, and help us to put that altruistic love into actions as described by St. Paul in 1 Corinthians 13.

AMENDS

Amends: something done to make up for injury caused

Purposely or inadvertently we do or say things that hurt our partner. A once popular song says "You only hurt the ones you love." We say critical and demeaning things. We treat the other person with condescension. We take our loved one for granted. We ridicule and belittle our mate in the presence of others. We yell in anger. We tease disrespectfully. We nag, withhold compliments and words of thanks, and ignore the one we said we would always cherish. We do things that violate our commitment to faithfulness, and we lie. Some are guilty of verbal or physical or mental abuse. Some abuse alcohol or other drugs. We forget birthdays and anniversaries. We cause hurt in so many ways.

What often follows the hurtful situation is a distancing, an icy atmosphere, an unbearable silence between the offender and the one who was hurt. The silence, the distance, and the iciness can go on for days. By the time the thawing has occurred and the silence and distance have ended, the couple may have forgotten what the hurt was, or they choose not to talk about the hurt. Instead they bury the injury without making any effort to prevent that hurt from happening again.

These ways of not dealing openly with the hurt are wrong, destructive, unhealthy, and not the way to achieve an A+ marriage! The hurtful words or actions need to be faced head-on as soon as possible. After the offended person has fully expressed thoughts and feelings about the hurt, it is absolutely essential that the offender offer apologies, and then make amends. To say "I'm sorry" is not enough. Words are not enough. Of course the best kind of amends is not to hurt again. But making that change may happen only over time, and only over time will the one who has been hurt see that the change in behavior is an authentic and lasting amending of the hurtful words or actions.

Immediate amends can help to heal wounds, as long as they are genuine. Phony, hypocritical, manipulative amends are not amends at all. Genuine amends are those that come from the heart, and are sincere signs of one's remorse and intention to change. A written letter of humble apology and sincere promise to refrain from the hurtful act or words, coupled with words of love and appreciation can be an effective way to make amends. A gift, a special date, tender demonstrations of affection, doing a task that's been on the "To Do" list forever, are all ways to make amends. Whatever the amends are, they must be sincere, honest, genuine, and above all, must be followed by elimination of the hurtful ways.

For discussion: When I do or say something that is hurtful to you, what kind of amends would you like me to make? Will you tell me when I unknowingly have hurt you? Will you be non-defensive when I tell you that I felt hurt by what you said or did, and will you try to understand me?

Prayer: When we have hurt our beloved, help us to acknowledge the wrong done, make amends, and restore intimacy and trust by changing our hurtful ways. Amen

AMIABILITY

Amiable: agreeable, friendly, sociable, congenial

No one is friendly and congenial all the time. Everyone is subject to low moods, depression, and times of being a pain in the you know what. The cause may be a monthly physiological female occurrence, or an annual demanding and stressful time on the job. But for a marriage to thrive and be healthy, both partners need to keep those disagreeable times to a minimum. Who wants to live with a chronic complainer, or with someone who is perpetually angry or down in the dumps or constantly negative? Yet some people seem to think that at home they have a perfect right to be disagreeable, unfriendly, uncommunicative, and downright nasty at any time, or even all the time. They are not like this anywhere else, but at home it's as if they become a different person. You could call them street angels and home devils. Where does the notion come from that in public we have to be cordial, congenial, and the life of the party, but in the privacy of home we can be grumpy, cantankerous, and a party pooper?

However you answer that question, now is the time to rethink, reconsider, and reorient. It is just as important to be amiable at home as it is on the job, at church, at the club, or at the home of friends. Maybe more important! Again, there will be times when we're bummed out, reclusive, and not exactly fit to live with. A word of explanation to the spouse would be in order, and a request for some quiet time alone would be appropriate. But to let this anti-social behavior go on indefinitely is unacceptable. If after making serious attempts to overcome the negativity, the depression persists, it may be time to seek medical intervention. But usually we can slowly bring ourselves out of our dumps and pits, sometimes by simply reminding ourselves to do an attitude check, sometimes by writing down what's bothering us, sometimes by sharing our concerns with our spouse, sometimes by praying, sometimes by going for a walk, sometimes by watching a humorous movie. Whatever works, do it!

If you are or your mate is subject to very radical mood swings, such as one day or one week or one month being highly animated, super energetic, and ultra amiable, but then suddenly becomes the very opposite for a period of time until you notice another dramatic mood swing, then medical intervention is not only desired but definitely required. No one wants to or needs to live with such marked changes in mood and behavior, and no one should be expected to live happily with someone whose behavior is so radically unpredictable. Help is available. Seek it, and then do what the doctor orders.

For discussion: What should I do and say when you're in a low mood that results in your being unfriendly and unsociable? What do you think that you could do to get yourself out of such a mood?

Prayer: Lord Almighty, enable me to be as amiable at home as I am in other settings. And if I have serious and long-lasting mood swings that go from being extremely energized to being acutely depressed, give me the courage to seek medical counsel. And if my spouse is subject to mood swings, grant me wisdom and strength to respond in ways that will be helpful. Amen

AMIGOS

Amigos: friends (Spanish)

Perhaps the highest compliment that can be paid to one's spouse is that he or she is your *best friend*. Relationships change as circumstances change, and each change presents challenges to that relationship. But if the friendship between the two remains constant, those challenges can be met. Deep and lasting friendship can overcome the challenges that changes always present. Those challenges include the addition of children to the marriage, increased job responsibilities, different political or religious beliefs, serious illness, the death of a child, long distance moves, absence for military duty, return from war, aging and its many consequences, infidelity, the loss of a job, the "empty nest," etc. These changes come with a multitude of challenges, and adapting successfully when these changes occur depends largely on how deep and solid a couple's friendship is. The saying is true that love conquers all, but it's true only if that love includes a strong and abiding friendship.

Much has been written on the subject of friendship. A friend is someone who accepts you just as you are. A friend is one who will stand by you when everyone else has abandoned you. A friend is a person who knows your every weakness, fault, and shortcoming, and still loves you. A friend enjoys being with you, listens to you, shares thoughts and feelings with you, genuinely likes you, understands your peculiarities, and encourages you to become all that you can be. A friend admires you, respects you, trusts you, cares deeply about your well-being, honors you, enjoys sharing time and activities with you, and does those things that are pleasing to you.

This is not to say that your mate should be your *only* friend. No one person can meet all the needs for social interaction of another person. Women need other women with whom to share common interests, and in whom they can confide. Men need other men who enjoy some things that their mate may not enjoy, and who like to talk about things their spouse isn't interested in. Most people understand and accept same gender friendships, but is it all right to have friends of the opposite gender? It is okay as long that friendship remains platonic and does not lead to romance and infidelity. One way to prevent a friendship from becoming a romance is to avoid situations in which the two friends are alone together, whether it be an "innocent" after work drink, or a lingering conversation about one's displeasures and dissatisfactions regarding one's marriage, or an intimate sharing of one's chemistry for that friend. If those things occur, or are likely to occur, they are bright red warning flags, telling you in no uncertain terms that it's time to change that friendship or end it!

For discussion: How do you define "friend?" Am I your best friend? What can we do to make our friendship stronger? Do you think that it's all right to have friends of the opposite sex? What are the risks involved in such friendships?

Prayer: Dear Friend above all friends, help us to deepen our friendship so that our friendship will prevail over any and all challenges that may confront us. Amen

AMOROUS

Amorous: full of showing love

When a loving relationship is new and fresh, showing love to one another is easy, frequent, and natural. Over time, many couples become less and less amorous, and the showing of love often becomes limited to infrequent bedroom sex that is somewhat routine. Even kissing among some couples becomes just a good-bye peck on the cheek. Routine same old, same old, as well as inevitable changes such as the addition of children, the greater pressures of work, the tendency to take one another for granted, the hectic pace of everyday responsibilities, plus unresolved problems are all among the many culprits that cause couples to be less and less amorous.

To be amorous can take many forms. A lingering good-bye or hello kiss on the lips, a ten second hug coupled with a kiss on the neck, a softly spoken eye-to-eye "I love you," an unexpected gift, a willingness to put down the newspaper or turn off the TV when a spouse wants to talk, a hand-written note that expresses love, holding hands while out together, a surprise candlelight dinner on a night when the kids are at a sleepover, a word of affection and affirmation such as "You are both beautiful and bright," or "I'm so glad that I have you in my life," or even just sitting together on the couch watching TV and cuddling during the commercials.

Large numbers of women wish that their husband would be more amorous *outside* of the bedroom. And maybe as many wish that their spouse would be *more* amorous *in* the bedroom, instead of hurrying through the act of love-making. Marriage counselors often hear women say "I feel used rather than loved when all it amounts to is 'wham-bam-thank-you-maam.'" To be amorous in love making means to go slowly, to pleasure each other, to whisper sincere words of affection, to caress gently, to be playful, to kiss every inch of the loved one's body, to be considerate, and to learn what the partner likes and doesn't like.

To achieve and maintain an A+ marriage, couples need to be amorous, i.e. need to be full of showing love to one another. Without these expressions of love each of the partners will feel unloved, taken for granted, used, and neglected. Years ago, a popular song entitled "Little Things Mean a Lot" was a reminder that to be amorous doesn't mean only to be sexual. A tender touch, a lingering kiss, an attentive listening ear, a breakfast in bed, an acknowledgement of genuine empathy, a kind word, a loving cuddle after sex — all of these little things expressed sincerely are ways of being amorous, i.e., examples of showing that the one doing them is full of showing love.

For discussion: What do you think it means to be amorous? What would you like me to do that shows my love for you? How could we make our love making more satisfying and exciting?

Prayer: Source of all love, help us to show love and affection more often and more openly. Give us the desire to be more amorous, and then enable us to act on that desire in ways that will strengthen our marriage and bring us closer to one another. Amen

AMUSEMENT

Amusement, amuse: to cause to laugh or smile by giving pleasure

Life can be stressful. Life comes with countless challenges, problems, decisions, and disappointments. So who wants a partner who's a grump? Who wants to be with someone who is chronically negative, who always sees the glass half empty rather than half full, who never tells a joke, and who rarely laughs or even smiles. Was that person born without a sense of humor, or did he or she lose it somewhere along the way? During courtship, he may have been the life of the party, but between then and the honeymoon, his funny-bone and sense of humor broke or became withered up and disappeared.

Some people grow up in a family where the unspoken mottos are "Life is not for fun;" "Marriage is not for fun;" "The family is not for fun." The person brought up in such a home may quite naturally take these mottos or themes into his or her adult life and into marriage and family life. If challenged he or she may respond with such words as "What's so amusing about unpaid bills?" "What's so funny about an increase in property taxes?" "What's so humorous about having to buy a new clothes dryer?"

"Where's the fun in painting the house?" "Taking care of a sick kid isn't exactly hilarious!"

If the adults in your childhood, including your preschool years were chronically unhappy, and taught you by their example that life is not for fun, you would probably decide that if you were to fit in with that family, you needed to adopt that theme or motto of "Life is not for fun." It's as if those influential giants in your pre-school years wrote the theme of your life, and then you unknowingly adopted that theme as your own. But it's never too late to change and rewrite the basic and underlying theme of what your life is going to be. If your life theme is something like "Don't be happy," or "Life is not for fun," and if you're an adult, you can adopt a different life theme or life script. An adult cannot blame his upbringing solely on those influential giants of his childhood. Maturity means to move forward by changing those themes or mottos that take the joy out of life. You may need help to change, and help is available. See a counselor or a life coach, or a psychologist who is knowledgeable about the impact of life scripts/themes/mottos.

Life without amusement is not amusing. Life without laughter is no laughing matter. Life without fun is not funny. Because life is serious, at times difficult, and has its share of disappointments, all the more reason to lighten up, laugh, and find amusing things to do. The people who enjoy life the most are those who can find humor even in life's quirks, glitches, bumps, bruises, and roadblocks.

For discussion: What did you learn from your family during your childhood about what your attitude about life ought to be? If what you learned is preventing you from being happy and enjoying life, what are you willing to do about changing that life motto/theme/ script? What could we do to bring more fun, joy, and laughter into our marriage?

Prayer: You made us with the capacity to laugh, to enjoy, to have fun. And you want us to have an abundant, full, joyful life. Thank you for fun and laughter. Help us to be able to play and laugh and enjoy the wonder and beauty of living. Amen

APHRODISIAC

Aphrodisiac: an agent that arouses or is thought to arouse sexual desire

Many foods and drugs are believed to increase a person's sexual desire. Most are not as effective as the legends and myths about them would have us believe. Of course, the use of alcohol and other street drugs often reduce inhibitions so that the person under the influence of these may uncharacteristically engage in sexual activity. But alcohol and street drugs are not aphrodisiacs.

The best aphrodisiac is a healthy, loving, genuinely caring relationship. The most effective sexually arousing agents are the people in a relationship, and the way they relate to one another. Ask women what they desire regarding sex, and most will say that they want communication. They want to be able to talk openly with their partner. They want their partner to share thoughts and feelings, and to listen attentively and respectfully to their thoughts and feelings. They also want a sense of humor in their lover. Additionally they want tenderness, and long and gentle foreplay. They want to be able to express openly what they like and don't like in bed. They don't want their partner to become defensive when they tell him that certain things turn them off, and that they would prefer certain other things instead. They want demonstrations of affection that are not always simply a prelude to intercourse. They want to be hugged, kissed, and affirmed verbally without thinking that these words and actions are simply a prelude to using her for his sexual satisfaction. Most women also want an afterglow of cuddling instead of him turning away immediately and going to sleep.

69

Most men are different. Men seem to be wired for sexual involvement, and are "hot to trot" without a lot of need for arousal. But men also want their aphrodisiac to be their lover. They don't want sex to be a duty for their spouse. They don't want fake orgasms. They want to be affirmed as good lovers. They sometimes want her to be the initiator of love making. Men often like to try a variety of places and sexual positions for intercourse, and appreciate it when their loved one is willing to experiment. However, if one or the other has moral, ethical, religious, or other strong personal objections to certain kinds of sexual acts, those objections need to be respected and honored.

Since the Creator fashioned and made human sexuality, and saw that it was good, we can say with certainty that sex is good. Unfortunately it can be made to be very bad. If a person has been sexually abused or raped as a child or as an adult, sexual problems will result. In such cases, not only is the non-abused person to be sensitive, patient, and understanding, but the abused person may be well-advised to seek professional and spiritual intervention.

For discussion: What is the very best aphrodisiac that truly "turns you on? Do you have any objections to sexual experimentations or to certain common sexual acts?

Prayer: Lord, You created human sexuality and saw that it was good. Help us to enjoy *our* sexuality, and assist us in making our sex life satisfying, fun, and bonding, even as we go through inevitable changes and challenges throughout the years of our marriage. Amen

APPRECIATION

Appreciation: recognition of value, quality, significance of another.

Everyone has a need to be appreciated. No one wants to be taken for granted. We want to be encouraged by being recognized as a person of value, quality, and significance. Yet, in many marriages, words and actions of appreciation are not often given. Couples become accustomed to a routine of role responsibilities, and consequently take one another for granted without giving each other words of appreciation. She drives the children to school, to Scouts, to dance lessons, to soccer practice, to youth group, and wherever else they need to go. That becomes her job, and neither the kids nor her husband ever express appreciation for her being chauffeur and taxi driver. He works forty or fifty or sixty hours a week, but instead of hearing that his long hours and the income he earns are appreciated, he's told that he works too much, or that he should ask for a raise.

The Bible tells us to "encourage one another and build each other up" (1 Thessalonians 5:11). Those are wise words of counsel. Words of appreciation encourage us and build us up. Yet some people think that if someone needs words of appreciation, that person is immature or suffers from poor self-esteem. That is nonsense! Just as we never outgrow our need to be loved and to be told that we are loved, we never outgrow our need to be appreciated, especially by those we cherish, but also by those for whom we work as employees. I know, however, that bosses, supervisors, and managers rarely tell their employees that they are appreciated. If a staff member suggests that the supervisor show more appreciation to those who work under him/her, that supervisor may respond by saying, "Why should I show appreciation when they're just doing the job that they were hired to do. I'm not here to hold their hands." (True story from my own experience.)

Then the employee goes home, but instead of hearing that he's appreciated, he hears about all the things on the "To Do" list that aren't done yet. She comes home from work, and instead of hearing that she's appreciated for holding down two full-time jobs – employee and homemaker – she hears that dinner is late or that the living room is a mess. What's so hard about giving a word of appreciation? What's so difficult about expressing a word of encouragement? What's the blockage that prevents us from saying something that builds up another person? Are we afraid that words of appreciation will spoil the one to whom we give those words? Do we fear that the recipient of appreciation will become conceited or lazy?

Words of appreciation are appreciated, even if the recipient of the appreciation acts as if he or she doesn't appreciate them. And if you have difficulty giving or receiving words of appreciation, you and your marriage would benefit greatly if you learned to give sincerely and to accept graciously.

For discussion: Do you agree that all people need to know that they are appreciated? Why is it important to be given expressions of appreciation? What could we do to improve both the giving and the accepting of expressions of appreciation?

Prayer: Father God, help us not to take each for granted, but to express appreciation to one another.

APPROVAL

Approval: favorable attitude or opinion

Because children look for approval from parents, teachers, and peers, some people think that the need for approval is childish, and that mature adults should not seek approval. But the need for approval is not evidence of immaturity or childishness. We never outgrow out need for the approval of others, especially the approval of those with whom we are the closest. From earliest childhood we hear words of disapproval. "No, no, bad, bad." "That grade you got this last marking period is not acceptable." "Your handwriting is awful." "You are stupid." "You are a monotone." "You're a mama's boy." "You're a loser." "Why can't you get the kind of grades that your sister got?" "Don't talk back to me young man."

Unfortunately, disapproval goes on through every stage of life. "No you're not good enough to make the team." "You didn't pass the test." "I don't approve of the music you listen to." "I'm not paying for your tuition, only to have you flunk your English class." "I'm sorry but you weren't selected for the college choir." "Thanks but no, I don't want to go out with you again." "In your annual appraisal, I've indicated that your performance is average, but I expect more from you in the future." "I appreciated our interview, but I didn't select you for the position." "Dad you're so predictable and boring." "Mom, get off my back!"

Even when not hearing disapproval from others, we're giving ourselves disapproval. "Why do I have to be so fat?" "I wish I could look like Cherry the cheerleader."

73

"I hate this acne!" "Why doesn't anyone ask me out for a date?" "I've sent out 50 resumes, had only two interviews and I'm still unemployed." "I've had this job for years, but have had just two small raises."

It's no wonder that we need approval! We need to hear that someone thinks that we're the greatest! We need to feel and to know that someone adores us! We need to believe that we are approved of mightily! We need to know that we have someone's unconditional approval.

We may never say to our partner, "You have my unconditional approval," or "I approve of you," but we can show approval by saying things like: "You are such a good parent," or "such a wonderful friend to me and to others," or "I really like the way you write," or "you sure are a good cook," or "I'm so very happy that you're in my life." or "you look so beautiful (or so handsome) in that dress (or that suit)," or "that company is very fortunate to have you as one of its employees," or simply "you're the best!"

For discussion: How would you like me to show that I approve of you?

Prayer: God of approval, help each of us to find ways of saying and showing approval to our loved ones Amen

APOLOGIES

Apology: words of regret for an offense or accident

I know a man who acknowledged to me that he has never said, "I'm sorry." It would be difficult to be in a relationship with such a person. Everyone makes mistakes. Everyone offends. Everyone accidentally or purposely hurts others. The Bible says "all have sinned and fall short of the glory of God." (Romans 3:23) Everyone needs to be able to apologize, especially to the ones we love the most. A sure sign of maturity is the ability to say, "I was wrong. I'm sorry."

If a relationship is to remain healthy, strong, and enduring apologies will be an essential part of that relationship. Apologies thaw and melt the ice of a relationship that has been frozen by the actions or words of one or both of the parties. Apologies can mend and heal the brokenness of a relationship that has been wounded by a thoughtless word or deed. Scars may remain, but without apologies wounds remain, and wounds can fester and even poison a person's entire feelings for the other.

However, apologies can become meaningless when the same hurtful words or actions are repeated over and over again, followed by another apology, a hug and a kiss. He screams and yells profanities and ugly names at her. She cries. Five minutes or five hours or five days later he apologizes. They hug and kiss and all is forgiven. Two days or two weeks or two months later, he does the same thing. She cries. He later apologizes. They hug and kiss and he promises never to do it again. But he does it again, and again, and again.

This becomes a kind of dance with predictable steps. But nothing changes. Apologies need to be sincere, and need to be followed with changed behavior. The behaviors of both the offender and the offended need to change. Often the behavior of the offender will not change until that of the offended changes. She could say, "I've heard your apologies so many times, and I'm sure that you're sincere, but nothing changes. I'm not willing to play this game any longer. I want and I expect and I will settle for nothing less than a change in your behavior. If there's any way that I can help you change, I'm willing to do so. If I can't help you, and you can't change by yourself, then I expect you to get help from someone who *can* help you. If you don't change, the next time you yell profanities and obscenities at me, I will have to . . . ." But idle threats and idle promises don't work. You must mean it. "I apologize." Two little words that can restore. "I am sorry." Three little words that can renew. "Unless . . . I will . . . " Words that can motivate change.

For discussion: How easy or how difficult is it for you to apologize? What do you want after your spouse apologizes to you?

Prayer: Show us the way and give us the ability to be humble enough to apologize, and the strength to change our unacceptable words and ways. Amen

ARTICULATION

Articulation: the act of vocal expression

When just about anyone is asked, "What is essential in a marriage"? the answer almost always is "good communication." Although communication is conveyed non-verbally, good communication does require vocal expression. And even though verbal communication is not the end all and be all of a healthy marital relationship, expressing oneself with words, and listening attentively to the words of the other person are key components of an A+ marriage. Effective communication requires articulation, i.e. verbally sharing thoughts, feelings, ideas, opinions, hopes, dreams, likes and dislikes. Good communication requires that each person in the marriage be articulate in their speech, and communicate verbally with more than grunts or one word mumblings or in outbursts of anger.

Men seem to have a harder time articulating what they think and what they feel. Women seem to have an easier time sharing words with another person, whether that be their spouse or a friend. Women often say that they wish their husband would talk more, and especially would share his feelings more openly. Whether it's nature or nurture that makes it more difficult for a man to articulate, i.e. to express himself verbally, is really beside the point. The point is that for a relationship to work, both individuals in that relationship need to be able to talk to the other in self-disclosing ways. No relationship will be lastingly satisfying and fulfilling if there is little or no open and honest sharing of words that help the other person to understand who their partner is.

Communication is a combination of two words – common and union. If there is to be a common union between two people, verbal communication is essential. To achieve an A+ marriage, effective articulate communication through frank, open, and honest sharing is imperative. Does your spouse know what you think and feel is the purpose of your life? Do you know what your mate thinks and feels about her or his experiences during military service? When your beloved's parent or some other favorite relative or friend dies, will you know what he/she is feeling? If your child gets in trouble or does poorly in school, will you articulate only your anger and disappointment, or will you also share your fears and worries? Have you ever shared with your spouse, or has your spouse ever shared with you what he or she likes and doesn't like sexually? If your partner were to become terminally ill, would you know what his or her wishes were regarding treatment, mechanical life support, preferences for place of care and death, e.g. hospital, care center, hospice, or home? If your spouse were to precede you in death, would you know what he or she would like with regard to a funeral or memorial service, burial or cremation, organ donation, beneficiaries, etc.? Have the two of you worked together on having a will?

For discussion: Why is it difficult to share verbally what we're thinking and feeling? What could I do to make it easier for you to talk openly with me? Do you think that open communication is essential? What do you think about sharing our thoughts about terminal illness and about death?

Prayer: Lord God, You created us with the ability to talk. Help us to articulate openly, honestly, and lovingly with one another. Help us to listen to one another with empathy, compassion, and kindness.

ASSERTIVENESS VS. AGGRESSION

Assertiveness: confident self-assurance in expressing oneself

Aggression: angry or violent behavior or speech

Aggressive behavior, including speech, is almost always destructive in any close personal relationship. Aggressive bosses produce disgruntled, unhappy employees. Aggression in a friendship results in alienation, if not in termination of that friendship. Certainly in marriage, aggressive behavior is never effective in long-term problem resolution. Whether the aggression is physical or verbal, it is never productive because aggression generates either fearful withdrawal or retaliatory aggression. Neither is conducive to building or strengthening a healthy intimate relationship. The aggressor may think he or she has had the last word and has won the battle, but the truth is that aggression results in a widening breach between the couple. Angry words and angry actions that accuse and demean the other do not solve or resolve anything, but only cause resentment and distance. Perhaps the only situation in which aggressive behavior is effective and even necessary is in military boot camp where the drill sergeant is charged with the responsibility of molding and making independent minded young men and women into highly disciplined soldiers who must learn to follow orders.

Assertiveness is different. To be assertive is to express one's thoughts and feelings in a spirit of self confident openness and honesty, but without hostile and critical put-downs. To be assertive is to be confidently straightforward, bold, authentic, and truthful, while maintaining civility and respect for the other person.

Soap operas and political debates show us examples of aggressive interactions in which angry raised voices hurl accusations, lies, and half-truths back and forth between foes. Unfortunately we don't have many examples in the media of open and honest *assertiveness* demonstrated by those of different opinions. Occasionally, comedic sit-coms show two people engaging in assertive exchange, and sometimes a Dr. Phil or a political commentator engage in assertive dialog with a person of an opposite viewpoint. But we are not taught in school or church or even at home how to be assertive without resorting to aggression. Often we are taught the opposite by the example of others in those places and certainly by what we see in movies and on television.

Aggressive behavior in a situation of differences: "You are stupid and lazy! Either shape up or get out!"

Assertive behavior in the same situation: "I've asked you to (do whatever), but you haven't done it. I'm feeling bad because it seems as though my requests are being ignored. I'd like us to talk about this."

For discussion: How would you explain the difference between aggression and assertiveness? What could we do to become more consistently assertive instead of aggressive?

Prayer: Kind and respectful Creator, enable and empower us to be assertive rather than aggressive. Help us to be consistently respectful, while being courageously open and honest with one another.

ASSURANCE

Assurance: a positive declaration intended to give confidence

Most of us, to one degree or another, lack full confidence in ourselves. We sometimes feel as if we're not as good a spouse as we ought to be. We compare ourselves with others, and are certain that we don't measure up. In our more honest moments, we admit that often we feel inadequate as lovers, as parents, as employees, as volunteers, and as adult offspring. We think we're too fat or too thin; that our nose is too big and our breasts too small; that we can't cook well; that our muscles are too small and our butt too big. When surveyed, about the only thing about which we think we're above average is as drivers! Just about all of us think that we're better drivers than others!

As self-confident as we may appear to others, beneath that façade of strength and healthy ego lies a deep insecurity and a fear of not being good enough. We need assurance and reassurance, especially from those who mean the most to us. We need compliments, positive reinforcement, and unconditional verbal, emotional and physical embraces that clearly declare "I think that you're wonderful!"

Yet, we are better at finding fault than in giving assurance. A boss is asked by his staff of ten to give them some words that they would find encouraging and uplifting, instead of only words that point out their shortcomings. He responds simply by saying, "I'm not here to hold your hand." That's sad, but fairly common in the workplace. Unfortunately, such an attitude is all too common in marriages and in families. We're quick to point out shortcomings in the other, but terribly slow to offer assurance.

No one is the perfect spouse or the perfect parent or the perfect cook or the perfect employee. No one has the perfect body, and no one is the perfect lover. If we think that we have to be perfect in our private lives, as well as in our public lives, we will be condemned forever to unhappiness, feelings of guilt, and an overwhelming sense of unworthiness. And if those closest to us rarely, if ever, offer us sincere assurances and reassurances, we are doubly cursed.

It's just as easy to say to your partner, "You handled that situation very well," as it is to say nothing or to suggest a better way of handling it. It's just as easy to say, "I really enjoy making love with you," as it is to say nothing at all. It's just as easy to say, "The stew was delicious," as it is to say, "Next time add some garlic." He may not admit it, but he wants to hear from you, "You are a super father!" She may not tell you, but she wants to hear you assure her that she's really smart. And beautiful. And a wonderful wife and mother.

Needing assurance is not a sign of weakness. Refusing to give assurance is.

For discussion: In what ways, and in what areas, would you like assurance from me?

Prayer: Almighty God, give us the will and the ways to give assurance sincerely and wholeheartedly. Amen

ASYLUM

Asylum: a refuge; sanctuary

We've heard the saying, "A man's home is his castle," but probably have never heard that a woman's home is her castle. Why not "A couple's home is their castle?" A couple's home is their refuge, their sanctuary, their safe retreat, their fortress, their asylum from the onslaughts and rigors of the working world. But what if he or she is the stay-at-home child-care provider and homemaker? Where is her or his asylum? It may have to be a date night, when a baby sitter provides respite so that the couple can get away for a relaxing evening together. It could be a quiet time alone when she can enjoy a soothing bubble bath without being interrupted by child or mate. It may be one night a week when he is out with the boys. Whatever form it takes, asylum is needed by everyone who carries a load of daily responsibilities, pressures, and deadlines.

Even though we know that a person's home is their castle, their fortress, their refuge, their asylum, we also know that all too often the home is not a fortress, not an asylum from life's skirmishes, but just a different battle-field in which volleys of ammunition, and bombshells of a different kind are the scenarios into which a person enters at the end of a work day, or in which a person feels trapped 24-7. She greets him at the door, not with a hug and a kiss, but with accusations and questions and complaints. Or he greets her with "Where the heck have you been?!" or "You should have seen what your son did today!" or "I've had it up to here with this Mr. Mom business!"

In all too many cases, the *workplace* becomes the asylum from the demands of the home and family, and the *home* becomes the war zone. Instead of the home being a castle, it becomes a curse. Instead of the home being an asylum, it becomes an insane asylum. Instead of being a refuge, it becomes a rifle range. Is it any wonder that about half of marriages fail? If there's no escape, no relief, no respite from constant demands and pressures, is it any wonder that so many are depressed and dissatisfied with life?

In order to achieve an A+ marriage, each couple needs to find ways to make their home a castle, a fortress, a sanctuary, a refuge, an asylum in which family members can be assured that this place called home will be a place of relief and refreshment. In order for that to happen, certain ground rules must be established and enforced. For example: a time limit put on griping and complaining, and time spent daily on sharing that day's joys and things for which each person is grateful. How about an agreed upon time alone for each partner every day. How about a fair and equitable sharing of household duties. How about time away together without children. How about being creative in coming up with ways in which to make your home a refuge for the weary, a sanctuary from the storms, an asylum in a world that sometimes seems insane.

For discussion: How could we make our home more of a safe and sane asylum?

Prayer: Help us to find ways to make our home a place of respite from life's battles. Give us the will and the way to include You as our Rest and our Renewal. Amen

ATTENTION

Attention: acts of courtesy or devotion indicating affection, as in courtship

Isn't it interesting that the example used in the above definition is "as in courtship?" Why not "as in marriage?" Do we stop paying attention after the courtship is over? Do we cease to engage in acts of courtesy or devotion that indicate affection once the wedding is history? Maybe so. Evidence: he's reading the newspaper while she's trying to talk to him; she's watching a TV soap opera while he's trying to get her attention about something that's important to him; she's checking her email, so "don't bother me" And if he's watching a football game on TV, heaven forbid if she should want his attention for anything less than that the house is on fire!

Of course some leeway can be given if your partner is deeply engrossed in a movie or a football game or in reading a book. Nor we would we interrupt someone who is on the phone or deeply involved in a person-to-person conversation. And it is aggravating to be expected to come to attention during the most critical part of the movie or the book or the game. But maybe you and your spouse could devise a way of conveying to your partner that you want his or her attention whenever there's a commercial or the end of a chapter or a lull in the action. And maybe a signal could be agreed upon that the signaled request was received, and that attention will be forthcoming.

Attention means an act of courtesy indicating affection. And the most basic act of courtesy is to stop what you're doing, make eye contact, listen with careful attention, and respond with genuine interest. To pay attention means to notice even little things like a new outfit, a different hairdo, a weight loss, an accomplishment or achievement. Attention can even mean a hug, a kiss, a compliment, a genuine and sincere "I love you."

A frequent complaint heard by marriage counselors is: "He doesn't pay attention to me any more." Or "She doesn't want to hear about my work like she used to." And, of course, that lack of attention is interpreted to mean, "He/she doesn't really love me any more. I'm just a take-for-granted fixture now."

Why is it that we tend to be more attentive to business associates than to our marriage partner? Why do we pay closer attention to friends than to spouses? If she's at a meeting or luncheon with girl friends, she wouldn't think of texting during that time. If he's at a business meeting with his boss and colleagues, would he be reading a newspaper?

Maybe we simply need to be reminded that attention is an act of courtesy that indicates affection, as in courtship. Maybe we need to heed the words of the once popular song, "Try to Remember." Try to remember how we paid attention during our courtship. Try to remember how we listened, and how we responded. "If you remember, then follow, follow, follow." Follow that way of being attentive.

For discussion: What are some ways you want me to give you attention? What signal could we use to indicate that we need attention when the other is deeply engrossed in something?

Prayer: We need help! We want to be attentive to each other. Help us to pay attention. Amen

AUTHENTICITY

Authenticity: real; not false

If there's anyone who wants you to be real, it's your spouse. If you can't be authentic with your partner, you're in for an uncomfortable and unsatisfying relationship. In so much of life we have to be somewhat inauthentic. We have to dress a certain way even if we hate wearing neckties, or despise high heel shoes. We have to be careful about our appearance, our language, our non-verbal communication, and what we reveal about ourselves. Shy introverts who work with the public have to learn to compensate for their preference to spend quiet time alone. Outgoing extroverts who work with the public have to learn when to stop talking and start listening. With most people, you don't wear your feelings on your sleeve, and you don't let it "all hang out."

Hopefully, at home you can be yourself. Hopefully, you have the freedom to be authentic. Hopefully, you won't want to be phony, and will not put on a false front. That is not to say that we are free to act any way we choose to act, or to say anything we want to say. If we have trouble managing anger appropriately, we still don't have permission to vent our anger at home in destructive ways. But if we come home angry or hurt or upset, we need someone with whom we can express those feelings authentically and appropriately. When an introvert comes home after dealing with people all day, he or she really may need some time alone to re-energize. But that introvert should let the spouse know that a brief quiet time alone is needed, and ought not to be interpreted as a sign of rudeness or as an indication of being anti-social.

However, if the real you is a slob or a demon in disguise, to be authentic doesn't mean that you have permission to be a slob or a demon anywhere in the home at any time, especially if your mate doesn't appreciate your being a slob or a demon. Or if the real you is chronically late, and your partner prefers to be early, you don't have permission to remain chronically late by claiming your right to be the real, the authentic you. Marriage gives us a relationship in which we can be authentic, but also gives us a relationship in which we can grow and become better marriage partners and more of what the Creator intends for us to be. Authenticity means being real, honest, open, and having your words and behaviors in sync with who you claim to be, or who you have convinced your beloved that you are. Phoniness in marriage doesn't fly well. My grandmother married a phony who in the days of their courtship presented himself as a religious social drinker. In fact he was an anti-religion abusive alcoholic. Prior to marriage, he put on a false front. After marriage he stopped his charade. Unfortunately, his authentic self was not an ideal marriage partner. Being authentic doesn't give us the freedom to act any way we want to act. Authenticity means being real and being honest, while simultaneously growing and becoming more and more the caring, kind, and compassionate husband or wife that we are created to be in marriage.

For discussion: What does being authentic mean to you? What doesn't it mean?

Prayer: Help me to be the real me, the authentic me that You and that my spouse want me to be. Amen

AUTONOMY

Autonomy: self-determination

When the Bible speaks of a man and a woman becoming one, it doesn't mean that one gives up his or her self-hood, self-determination, and individuality. Marriage is not intended to be an institution in which one's person-hood is surrendered. Even though the Bible says that "the husband is the head of the wife just as Christ is the head of the church," we need to remember that what some use as a proof-text to show that God intends for the man to rule over the woman, the text continues by saying that the man is to love his wife as Christ loves the church, and *gave* himself for it. To be the head of the wife, therefore, does not mean dominance, but rather self-sacrificing unconditional love in a relationship of equality in which both husband and wife retain their God-given autonomy, but in such a way as to honor and respect one another.

We also hear stories and jokes about how the husband might *think* that he's the head of the household, but he *knows* and everyone else knows, that the wife is really the "boss," and she's the one who rules the roost. Does a marriage have to have a ruler or a boss? Even in work settings where there are managers and supervisors, employees are more satisfied and more productive when they are given a voice in decision-making, and where their individuality is respected and their opinions solicited. Few, if any people really enjoy being just a "yes man," or a "yes woman" whose ideas, input, and independence are not taken seriously. Perhaps there are marriages in which one or the other of the spouses truly wants to be subservient, and enjoys taking orders

89

from headquarters. If that's the case, and it works, so be it. But if such an arrangement of one being the boss and the other a passive servant doesn't work, then that arrangement needs fixing, and the repair needs to be such that autonomy is preserved for each spouse, and leadership is shared equally.

When a marriage becomes a power struggle to see who's going to be the head honcho, war will eventually erupt. And war always results in serious casualties to the combatants, as well as to the non-combatant collaterals, i.e. the children. Even after a viable solution is reached between husband and wife, skirmishes may occur from time to time. But a skirmish can be resolved without serious injuries, and a lasting truce can be reached as long as respectful autonomy is granted to each, and each takes mature responsibility in the problem-solving process.

For discussion: What ought autonomy look like in our marriage? If we were making a video that showed autonomy as a characteristic of our marriage, what would we be doing and saying? When we are having a discussion during which we disagree, how can we retain our individual autonomy without being offensive, and without one or the other simply becoming a passive, angry, patsy?

Prayer: Give us the will and the way to figure out how to make autonomy work effectively in our marriage. Lead us, guide us, and give us wisdom to find ways to respect and honor each one's individuality and right to express opinions, even when we disagree. Amen

ACTIONS TO AVOID

ABASHING

Abash: to destroy the self-confidence of; make embarrassed or ashamed

She took a painting class and completed a picture that she thought was pretty darn good. She was pleased enough with it to frame it and hang it in the family room where it hung for about a week. Then it disappeared. Some days later she found it stashed in the back of a basement closet. Her husband was the culprit. She never again took a painting class or tried her hand at developing any latent artistic talent she may have had.

How do you respond to that kind of wordless criticism? She retaliated by finding fault with his income, his laziness about domestic responsibilities, his ways of relating to the children, and especially *his artistic passion* – photography. She bashed him so he bashed her. Not only is it rude and inconsiderate to abash another, but it is highly destructive in a marriage relationship.

We get enough put-downs and bashings outside the home. We don't need any more inside the home. What we need is encouragement, compliments, praise, and frequent pats on the back. "Good job," "I think it looks good," "That's really neat," "Wow!," and "You continue to surprise me with your abilities," are marriage-builders. Abashings are marriage busters. And we are our own worst critics. We find fault with so much of what we do. "I cooked the meat too long." "I should have said this instead of that in my speech." "I screwed up a word in my solo." "I was too harsh with Johnny today." Even after receiving compliments, we have a tendency to find fault with ourselves. So we really don't need our spouse to add to the destruction of our self-confidence.

The old saying is "If you can't say anything good, don't say anything at all." Putting that saying into practice may be better than openly bashing, but it doesn't take a particularly perceptive genius to figure out that if someone says nothing, it means that they think the effort stinks, and they can't find a single good thing to say about it. Say something positive first, and then tact-fully make comments or suggestions.

Abash also means to make embarrassed or ashamed. How do you feel when a spouse makes fun of his or her partner in the presence of others? How do you feel when your spouse thinks he's being funny by "teasing" you about your dieting or your scrapbooking or your art lessons or your poetry? It's not funny to you. You feel embarrassed or ashamed. Publicly criticizing another person, especially one's spouse, is cruel, unkind, and uncalled for. Just don't do it!

The Bible tells us to encourage one another and build each other up. That's good counsel for couples to follow. Be a builder, not a basher!

For discussion: What up-building words would you like to hear from me?

Prayer: Lead us, guide us, and enable us to be builders instead of bashers. Amen

ABUSE

Abuse: n. act of treating a person or object improperly or wrongly

Abuse of another person can take many different forms:

Physical abuse, including bodily harm, sexual demands/actions, and neglect;

Verbal abuse, including name-calling, insidious teasing, demeaning joke-telling, and swearing;

Emotional abuse, including secret absences, excessive use of drugs, alcoholism, irresponsible spending, unwillingness to share in responsibilities, chronic absence of demonstrations of affection, and the silent treatment. Abuse can be violent or non-violent, active or passive, overt or underhanded, obvious or veiled, frequent or rare. Violent abuse includes hitting, slapping, pushing, and whatever else that causes physical pain or discomfort. Non-violent abuse could be neglect, "innocent" name-calling and criticisms, public joke-telling in which one's partner is the butt of the joke, withholding of affection, and ongoing refusals to give affirmations. Active, overt, and obvious abuse is up-front and outspoken, whereas passive, underhanded, and veiled abuse is subtle and cloaked in an air of innocence and denial when confronted. "I didn't mean anything by that! You're too sensitive!" "Can't you take a joke?!" "Why are you always so defensive?"

The perpetrators of abuse, as well as the abused, can be either male or female. The woman who is repeatedly abused says that she won't take it any longer, yet continues to come back for more of the same. The husband whose wife drinks excessively, or who demeans him in front of the children and others, or who openly engages in extra-marital involvements, complains about her behaviors, but takes no meaningful actions to deal with the issues. The reasons for such martyrdom can be many. Some people grow up in homes where abuse is the norm. Some are raised in environments that are not conducive to encouraging self-esteem. In either case, the individual thinks and feels that he or she doesn't deserve any more than they are getting. Some stay in abusive relationships for religious reasons, believing that the marriage vow "for better or for worse," means that no matter how bad the abuse gets, God wants them to stay in the relationship. Others remain the victims of chronic abuse because they fear that no one else would want them, or that on their own they couldn't manage financially.

Abuse in any form or shape or type is not acceptable, and will not result in a life-enriching relationship. Abuse is not part of God's plan for marriage or for any other relationship. Abuse is demonic, reprehensible, unfair, and uncalled for. Those who abuse and those who are abused, but who do nothing to change the unhealthy nature of their relationship, do no one any favors by continuing the abuse or by continuing to allow the abuse to go on. Children who see and experience abuse in their childhood homes are much more likely to be abusers and the abused in their adult relationships.

For discussion: Are there ways in which we are abusive to one another? If so, what shall we do?

Prayer: God of gentle caring, help us never to abuse our partner or anyone else.

ACQUIESCENCE

Acquiescence: agreement without protest

Often acquiescence has a negative connotation. Someone who acquiesces is thought of as a spineless wimp. If acquiescing is all that a person ever does, and never stands up to protest or to defend one's position or point of view, then that person may rightfully be a called a spineless wimp. And if all such a person does is give in, cave in, freeze up and shut up, he or she will most likely end up being locked up. Why? Because such people often crack up and kill, or end up with a psychiatric diagnosis and hospitalization.

But as in all of life, so too in married life, people have to decide what is worth a fight, and what isn't worth fighting over. Often at some point in a marriage, there's a power struggle over who will have control. At that point, couples often fall into the trap of fighting over everything and every possible issue that arises. And all too often that's the reason that many marriages end within the first two years of the wedding. Marriages that endure are those in which both partners decide, whether consciously or not, that agreement without protest is often the best route to take in matters that are not all that crucial, and certainly not essential to one's self esteem, or to one's self image as a person with both a brain and a backbone.

For example, does it really matter if the toilet paper unrolls from the top or from the bottom of the roll? In *his* childhood home, the toilet paper always unrolled from the *top*, but *she* learned that it ought to unroll from the *bottom*. Rather than make it an issue on which the fate of the planet depends, why can't one of them acquiesce and save the knock-down, drag-out arguments for the truly significant issues of personal values and personal integrity. She wants Christmas presents opened on Christmas Day, but his family tradition has always been to open gifts on Christmas Eve. Is one right and the other wrong? Acquiescence on the part of one would be a far better choice than acting like a couple of stubborn children, each of whom insists on his/her way.

On the other hand, if he's a rotten money manager and sees no problems with always having a $10,000 credit card bill, she would be well-advised not to practice acquiescence in that situation. If she wants to live as if they had a champagne budget, even though they have a generic beer income, he had better not acquiesce over that disagreement. If one of the couple thinks that disciplining children is unwise and unnecessary, while the other is certain that undisciplined children will become spoiled brats and irresponsible adults, the disciplinarian ought not to give in. If she believes that drunkenness is not acceptable, but he thinks it's okay to come home drunk, she had better not acquiesce.

For discussion: What do you think is worth fighting for? When do you think we should acquiesce?

Prayer: Grant us patience and wisdom to decide when acquiescence would be better than a long drawn-out battle. And give each of the strength to fight for those issues that are truly crucial, and help us to be willing and able to consent or to compromise.

ADULTERY

Adulterate: to pollute; to make impure

Adultery: voluntary sexual involvement between a married person and someone other than his or her spouse.

Adultery contaminates a marriage and any committed exclusive relationship. Adultery pollutes such relationships. When adultery happens, the relationship is contaminated with a lack of trust, with deep sadness, with unbelievable disappointment, with uncontrollable anger, with hurt that aches to the very core, with desires to get even, and sometimes with a raging hatred that will not forgive.

Why does adultery make a relationship impure? Why does adultery cause so much pain, so much fear, so much anger, so many tears? Why do we want marriage to be sexually exclusive? Why don't we want our partner to be involved sexually with anyone else? Why is it that we have no problem with our spouse having a working relationship with someone of the opposite gender, but don't want our partner involved in a sexual relationship with someone else? A person may even be unbothered by their partner dancing with another, or hugging another, or getting kissed on the cheek by another. But going to bed with another is a totally different matter. Why?

Because in our culture sexual intimacy is something extremely special, extremely private, and extremely personal. Even if one or both individuals in a committed relationship were sexually active with one or more lovers prior to marriage, they now expect that both will be sexually faithful. It's a unique bond, a sacred trust, a one-of-a-kind sharing of oneself, a holy encounter, a spiritual experience of tenderness and joy, a passion unlike any other, and a union of body and soul with that of body and soul that is without equal. It is the ultimate expression of love that we cherish beyond words, and do not want that deep and cherished love to be shared with anyone else. If it is, we feel cheated of a love that we believed was ours alone, and not something to be shared with anyone else.

When adultery occurs and is discovered, can trust be reestablished? Can the offended partner forgive? Can the relationship be restored? Yes, but only if certain and definite conditions are met. The adulterer must be contrite, sincerely ask for forgiveness, renew his or her vow of faithfulness, and be very, very patient with the one who has been betrayed. The one betrayed needs to understand that forgiveness does not mean forgetting, and does not mean approval of the adultery. Forgiveness means to set aside the urge to get even, the desire to hurt the offender, the seething anger, and the unwillingness to ever trust again. Forgiveness means to let go of a sense of moral superiority. But forgiveness takes time. And forgiveness takes determination. And forgiveness doesn't happen without divine help.

For discussion: Why is sexual faithfulness so important? If adultery happens, what should we do?

Prayer: Lord of love, help us to remain faithful to one another. If we adulterate, contaminate, and pollute our relationship with adultery, forgive us, and enable us to restore our relationship. Amen

ADVICE

Advice: an opinion or recommendation offered as a guide to action, conduct, etc.

She: "Honey, I'm worried about the job interview I have next week. I'm scared that I'll blow it."

He: "Don't be silly. Worry won't help anything. Just relax and be yourself. You'll do fine."

He: "Sweetheart, there's this guy at work who's always giving me a hard time. I'm sick of it, but he's one of the boss's golden haired boys who can do no wrong. I just don't know what to do."

She: "Well, just tell him off! Tell him to get off your back! Don't just take that kind of abuse! Stand up to him! Tell him firmly that you don't appreciate his remarks, and that you won't take it anymore!"

Advice is cheap, and unless we request it, we don't want advice! Yet, when a loved one confides in us, expressing a concern or quandary, we are quick to give advice. We think we have to come up with an answer or with a solution. We think an answer or a solution is what is being requested. It's not! The last thing we want from a confidant is an answer or a solution! When someone responds with "Well, this is what you should do," it makes us feel as if the answer-giver thinks we're so stupid that we couldn't come up with the answer. What we really want is someone who will listen attentively and with care not giving answers or solutions. We want someone who shows understanding, and who trusts that we will come up with the right answer or solution.

You may be familiar with the old saying "God gave us two ears and one mouth so that we would listen twice as much as we talk." We may even believe that saying, but it's a rare person who listens even half as much as he talks. We're not taught to be listeners. We are taught as infants how to talk, and later we take classes on public speaking, on how to make small talk, on how to talk during a job interview, on how to talk on the telephone, on how to talk on a first date, on how to talk as an actor, etc. But few people take classes on how to be a good listener.

In our jobs we have to give answers. As parents we need to give our children advice. As committee members, scout leaders, youth group advisors we are expected to have answers to questions, and solutions to problems. So we think that's our responsibility as a spouse. "My partner faces a tough decision and I'm supposed to give her advice." No, your partner doesn't really want advice. She wants you to listen with your full attention and with caring concern. "My partner expresses concern over a problem he's dealing with, and I truly believe that he's asking me to tell him how to solve that problem." No, he's not. He just wants you to listen with your complete attention, and to let him know that you have heard him compassionately and correctly. It's true that advice is cheap. Don't give it unless it's asked for. Instead listen, listen, listen.

For discussion: When you share a problem or concern with me, what would you like from me?

Prayer: Help us, O God, to listen with our ears and with our heart. Amen

AGGRESSION

Aggression: first act of hostility

Hostile actions do not resolve relational conflicts. Hostility either leads to an escalation of defensive anger, or causes the recipient of the aggression to withdraw into silence and passivity. Aggression is not the way to solve problems within a relationship. Aggression stifles creative problem solving, shuts off rational conversation, greatly impairs closeness, and ultimately destroys love. All intimate relationships have times of conflict and differences that can include fighting and arguing. However, couples have to learn to fight fairly, and being aggressive and hostile are not the ingredients of a fair fight.

Fair fighting has rules, just as prize fighting has rules. In the ring, boxers are not allowed to hit below the belt. In a committed relationship, being aggressive is "hitting below the belt." Aggression is against the rules. If aggression is allowed, hostile voices and hostile actions can easily escalate, and hostile speech and acts often result in physical and emotional abuse. Regularly we hear or read about a couple whose argument led to aggression that led to violence that resulted in a black eye or broken bones or a fatal stabbing. When aggression takes over, the rational and reasonable is wiped out, and the irrational reactive, non-thinking animalistic instincts and impulses reign exclusively.

The first step in eliminating aggression is to make a conscious commitment not ever to resort to aggressive behaviors. The person who is an angry aggressor must begin to recognize the thoughts and feelings that precede his or her aggression. Those precursors of aggression can be identified both by the aggressor and the person to whom the aggression is directed. The aggressor may feel a hot flash that goes through his body. The other person may hear an increase in the volume of the aggressor's voice. If either is experienced, a time out to gain control is needed.

Sometimes the person who repeatedly engages in aggressive behaviors needs professional help in learning anger management. And sometimes aggressive behaviors can be controlled through medication. Certainly, divine help can be highly beneficial if the individual is open to it, and will ask for it. Any and all possible means of stopping aggression must be brought into play or disastrous consequences are guaranteed. Physical harm will occur, police will be called, children who witness the aggression will be negatively impacted, a jail sentence could be imposed, and the odds of divorce are far greater than the odds for reconciliation.

Aggression is a killer, both figuratively and literally. It is not helpful in conflict resolution. It does not bring about a closer bond. It does not enhance intimacy. And it is not in accord with the will of the Creator. If a relationship is to succeed and thrive and be life-giving, aggression must not be allowed.

For discussion: Are either of us ever guilty of aggression? How can we help one another never to resort to aggression?

Prayer: Guide us in the ways of effective problem solving and creative conflict resolution. Help us to be totally committed to peaceful and fair means of fighting. Amen

ALCOHOLISM

Alcoholism: addiction to alcohol that causes problems in living

All addictions are detrimental and damaging to marriage and family life. Alcoholism is the most common form of addiction in America, and consequently causes more difficulties in relationships, and is the immediate cause of more divorces. A simple but accurate definition of alcoholism is easily remembered with the acronym WART – **With Alcohol Repeated Trouble**. What type of alcohol, how much alcohol, how often alcohol is consumed are not the issues when determining the disease of alcoholism. The only determinative issue is whether the use of alcohol leads to repeated trouble. The trouble could be a number of things: spousal or child abuse, citations for drunk driving, gambling that results in massive debt, infidelities, medical conditions, job firings, unexplained extended absences from home, arrests, automobile accidents, irresponsible spending that jeopardizes the family's finances, etc.

As with any addiction or disease, denial is the first response. "I don't have a problem! I can quit whenever I want to!" Denial is common even with other medical diagnoses. So it's understandable when a person denies that he or she is an alcoholic. If a loved one has seen repeated trouble resulting from another's drinking, it's time for a conversation with the one whose drinking has been problematic. One way is to ask four simple questions: Do you ever think that you should **CUT down** on your drinking? Do you ever get **ANGRY** when someone questions whether or not your drinking has become excessive or problematic? Do you ever feel **GUILTY about** your drinking or what you've done as a result of your drinking? Do you ever use alcohol as an **EYE opener** to help you get going in the morning? A simple way of remembering these questions is to take the first letter of each of these words – **<u>Cut</u> down**, **<u>Angry</u>**, **<u>Guilty</u> about**, **<u>Eye</u> opener** – **CAGE**. By initiating the conversation, you open the CAGE. If the one being questioned answers yes to one or more of the questions, that person's drinking is not normal social drinking. So, the idea is to open the CAGE and look for the WART.

Often a one-on-one conversation with the one whose drinking may have become problematic is not effective. Therefore a confrontation, often called an intervention, by the entire family and even friends may be called for. The confrontation includes specific examples of times when the drinking of the one being confronted has resulted in problems. The confrontation must also include a mandate that the problem drinker get help. The help may be an addictions treatment facility, and/or frequent (even daily) attendance at meetings of Alcoholics Anonymous. Whether or not the problem drinker/alcoholic seeks treatment, the immediate family members need to become involved in meetings that provide support for spouses and children. A recovering alcoholic who is the director of one state's alcohol intervention program said, "The hardest thing for anyone to do is to love an untreated drinking alcoholic." If that's true, then family members of one who suffers from alcoholism need all the help they can get.

For discussion: Has the use of alcohol or other drugs become a problem for us?

Prayer: Help us to be honest about our use of alcohol/drugs, and if there is a problem, help us. Amen

APATHY

Apathy: absence of passion, emotion, or excitement

The opposite of love is not always hate. More often in a marriage the opposite of love is apathy. One or both partners lose their passion, enthusiasm, and excitement about the relationship. The couple gets into a rut of boring familiarity, and simply go through emotionless motions of love. Eat, sleep, go to work, do necessary chores, watch TV, tuck the kids into bed, go to bed at different times, get up at different times, and start the whole routine over again. No surprises, no variations in routine, no meaningful conversations, no dates, no romance, and infrequent same old, same old sex. Apathy reigns. And when apathy reigns, apathy leads to all kinds of troubles, including depression, overeating, weight gain, chronic unhappiness, more time spent away from home, "innocent" affairs, adultery, and divorce.

Apathy is a killer. It stifles and smothers caring, empathy, spontaneity, demonstrations of affection, meaningful conversations, planning for the future, fun, laughter, and love making. Apathy also is detrimental to the children because kids sense acutely and accurately when their parents' relationship is not one of genuine love, but a sham of pretense and pretending. And apathy sets a deeply flawed and poor example of what marital love is to be.

Apathy often begins innocently enough. The honeymoon is over, the kids and the jobs take precedence, day to day life becomes routine, sex doesn't vary, and we think we know all that there is to know about our partner. Differences don't get resolved so they're not discussed any longer. Problems don't get solved so they continue to chafe, but are no longer a topic of conversation because previous talks about those problems never got anywhere. After a period of time, one or both begins to think "Is this all there is? Do I really love him or her? Did I make a mistake in choosing this person as my life partner?" But rather than try to work it out with open and honest communication, or with the help of a counselor, each decides to grin and bear it. Maybe it will get better when we have children. Maybe when the children are older. Maybe when the children leave home. Maybe when he's not so pressured at work. The result is apathy. No feeling, no fun, no friendship. Nothing but boredom and disinterest. Apathy can be avoided, but only with intentional resolve to kill it before it kills the relationship. Here are some things that couples can do to squash apathy before apathy chokes them.

1. Keep talking. Practice the guidelines of effective communication, i.e. saying "I think, I feel, I want:" listening intently and giving feedback of what you've heard; refraining from aggressive behavior.

2. Keep on doing the little things that mean so much, i.e. hugs, kisses, and words of affection, empathy, understanding, appreciation and compliments; remembering special days; love notes and letters; surprises, fun dates, and weekends without the kids; prayers for and/or with your partner.

For discussion: What would you like from me in order to prevent apathy.

Prayer: Help us to remember the excitement and enthusiasm we had early in our relationship, and to find ways of avoiding apathy by being creative and imaginative in keeping our love vibrant. Amen

ASSUME

Assume: to take for granted without proof

After knowing a person for awhile, we get to thinking that we know them well enough to be able to read his or her mind, know his motivations, understand her rationale for doing things, and can accurately predict their every preference, desire, and thought. We assume their reasons and rationale for actions, decisions, and conclusions. We take for granted without solid proof that we know this partner inside and out, forward and backward, upside down and right side up. We even think that we know this person better than she knows herself.

Of course, the longer we know a person, the better we get to know that person. What we forget is that the longer we know a person, the more we are subject to making assumptions about that person. We also forget that people grow and change, and that what once was true about them may no longer be true. It has been said that if we're going to remain married to the same person, we will need to remarry that person several times as they change with different stages of life. The young mother of two infants may change when those children go off to school, or grow up and leave home. The young and ambitious man whose dreams have been realized or shattered may become a different person with different interests and aspirations when he turns 35 or 40. And when this married couple become grandparents, we can't assume that their thoughts and hopes and ideals and interests will continue as always.

The old saying is that when I assume something about you, I often make an ass out of myself rather than be the all-knowing perceptive and sensitive person that I thought I was. You assume that because she's a home-maker she would love to get a vacuum cleaner from you on her birthday. She is a kind and sensitive person so she doesn't tell you that she's offended by such a gift, and would prefer something more personal and romantic. You assume that because he enjoys working in his wood shop, he would like a new set of screw-drivers for Christmas, when actually he was hoping for something less practical. He doesn't tell you what he would have preferred so you continue to assume that he always wants gifts like neckties, socks, and saw blades. To your partner, your assumptions make you look like an ass who really doesn't know you at all.

You may assume that your wife doesn't like sex, when in fact she likes sex, but doesn't like the way you go about having sex with her. She assumes that you'll get angry with her if she tells you what she'd prefer sexu-ally, so she keeps quiet. You may assume that your hus-band is an insensitive animal who thinks only of himself in bed, when in fact he wants very much to satisfy you, but since you don't share your desires, he assumes that you're just not all that interested. The only way to stop making an ass of yourself is to stop ass-uming and start communicating openly and honestly. Assume nothing.

For discussion: What assumptions do I make about you that are not correct?

Prayer: You know us, but we'll never fully know our-selves or our partners. Help us not to assume that we will, but rather to see one another as a mystery we'd like to get to know. Amen

ARROGANCE

Arrogance: an attitude of superiority manifested in an overbearing manner that comes from believing that you are better, smarter, or more important than other people.

Does anyone want a partner who believes that he or she is better, smarter, or more important than others, including the partner? Arrogance is not usually considered a virtue, especially in a marriage! Marriage is to be a partnership of equals. Even those who believe that they must take literally the biblical words that the husband is to be head of the wife ought not think that therefore the husband is entitled to arrogance.

I doubt that any marriage manual or any book on how to be successful in business or in society recommends that a person become arrogant. I doubt that any religion or philosophy of life encourages people to be arrogant. Unless a person's partner suffers from a major inferiority complex, and has an ongoing and overpowering need to continue to see himself or herself as inadequate and unworthy, arrogance in a marriage is eventually going to stifle and smother a marriage. Why? Because arrogance causes the other partner to feel inadequate, inferior, unworthy, child-like, despicable, and disposable. And when a person believes that he or she is superior to and more important than the partner, any word or action is acceptable to be used, including name-calling, infidelity, and physical abuse.

Marriage is intended to be a relationship in which each of the partners can grow and become more of their God-given potential. If a marriage doesn't enable each to develop and grow, then that marriage is not living up

111

to its purpose and ideal. Arrogance on the part of one or both partners does not encourage, nurture, or nourish the development of the other partner. Arrogance does the opposite.

Arrogance is not the same as healthy self-esteem. Often arrogance is a cover-up and defense for low self-esteem. Positive self-esteem is a highly desired quality, and is necessary for quality of life, as well as for a healthy marriage. But arrogance will not result in a good life or a good marriage. Humility, an awareness of one's strengths and weaknesses, and a high respect for a partner's strengths, virtues, capabilities, and unique personality are essential elements for a meaningful life and healthy marriage.

An arrogant person usually finds it difficult, If not impossible, to show empathy, kindness, thoughtfulness, or consideration for others. An arrogant person is typically self-centered, boastful, brash, demanding, and overbearing. He or she treats others with disrespect and condescension. Those characteristics and actions do not make for a lasting and satisfying marriage. All of us not only want and need but long for respect, kindness, encouragement, and the knowledge that we are cherished and regarded highly. If that isn't what you're giving your partner, you may need professional help.

For discussion: What do you want me to say or do if you are acting arrogantly?

Prayer: God, deliver me from arrogance. Help me to be humble, and to be able to encourage my partner with demonstrations of respect, appreciation, and high regard. Amen

ARCHEOLOGY

Archeology: the scientific study of historic or prehistoric peoples and their cultures by analysis of their artifacts, inscriptions, monuments and other remains.

In order to study artifacts and other remains of people from the past, archeologists must dig up those artifacts and remains. They dig up the past. Such digging is necessary in archeology, but in marriage, digging up the past is usually unproductive, often disastrous, and can be deadly, even to the extent of leaving only remains of a once healthy and thriving relationship. Avoid archeology; avert digging up the past.

The old saying, "Let sleeping dogs lie," ought to be the motto and watchword of every marriage. What's done is done, and cannot be undone. As long as the wrong done has been discussed openly, sincere apologies extended and accepted, and honest efforts made to change and to avoid repeating that wrong, no benefit can result from bringing it up again. If the wrong continues to be repeated, even after apologies and promises of reform, then the matter needs to be addressed. But if the offensive action is not repeated, digging it up again for whatever reason is going to be counter-productive.

Take for example the situation in which one or the other becomes so irate that he or she loses it, and resorts to physical violence. Maybe it's a slap or a push or a shaking or something worse, but it's totally unacceptable and perhaps even out of character. The offender is ashamed, makes sincere apologies, and never repeats that behavior. Weeks, months, years later, for whatever reason, the offended one digs up that incident and throws it in the face of the offender. The only things such digging up the past will accomplish are to make the offender defensive and angry. He or she will either retreat or retaliate, leave or level a defensive volley of words intended to point out the faults of the other by digging up the other's past sins and shortcomings. Now we're in a war that has no rules of fairness. Now anything goes. Voices get louder. Accusations become stronger. Other past offenses are dug up and thrown at one another. Soon the original reason for the discussion or argument is forgotten in the heat of battle. Bigger and bigger guns are brought out as character is assassinated, good qualities of the other are obliterated, and good will destroyed.

No relationship, no matter how strong, can withstand the onslaught of repeated archeological digs that bring up the undesirable actions of the past. Work it out, talk it out, get it resolved as soon after the offense happens. You may never forget the offense (forgiveness does not mean forgetting), but to dig it up and throw it up at the offender will never be an effective strategy in strengthening the relationship. Archeology in a marriage leads only to a relationship that ends up as bones and artifacts of what once was.

For discussion: How do you feel when I bring up some unacceptable behavior of yours from the past?

Prayer: Father, give us the capacity to forgive and to let the past be buried, never to be unearthed again. Amen

AVARICE

Avarice: Greed

A movie in the 90's had the character played by Kirk Douglas saying, "Greed is good," and then continued by strongly defending greed as the incentive and defining ingredient of what makes for a strong economy, a satisfied people, and a great nation. I would rather believe that ambition, creativity, a desire to realize one's potential, and a love for God, family, and country are the things that drive the economy, that make for a satisfied people, and that result in a great nation.

At any rate, greed in a marriage or in any committed relationship is not good. Avarice is the result of self-centeredness, and self-centeredness is a killer of any relationship, and is especially deadly in a marriage. Greed often leads to making one's career more important than the family. Greed can cause workaholism, meaning that a person is addicted to work, to advancement, to career, to making money. Greed is often the cause of massive debt. Greed leads people to want more and more and more, even if it means sinking deeper and deeper into credit card debt, even if it means paying the credit card company 20% interest, and even if it means that all that can be paid monthly is the interest.

Greed is what blinds people to financial common sense. Greed is what says "I want what I want when I want it." It doesn't matter whether or not what I want is what we can afford. Greed is what makes people think that they are entitled to whatever their neighbors have, even if they have an income that's only half of their neighbor's.

And greed is what prevents individuals and couples from giving to church and charities. Even though it's been demonstrated over and over again forever that it is more blessed to give than to receive, greed says that it's better to get than to give. Greed prevents people from discovering the joy of giving. Gimme, gimme, gimme seems to be the theme and motto of people who firmly believe that they are entitled to anything and everything that their heart desires.

A mentality of avarice is not willing or able to make sacrifices, even though sacrifices are often part and parcel of a successful relationship. "I want my way, or it's the highway." "What I want is far more important than what you or the family wants or needs." "You want to give away 10% of the earnings we bring home! Are you crazy?!" "I'm entitled to sex whenever I want it." "I'm entitled to a new car every two years." "I don't care how much it costs – I want a weekly house cleaning service!" "I'm going out with the boys every Saturday night, whether you like it or not!" "We're buying an annual concert pass, whether you're going with me or not." "Okay, and I'm buying an annual football pass whether you're going with me or not!"

For discussion: In what ways are we greedy? Is greed good or bad for our relationship?

Prayer: Generous giver of life and of grace, teach us and show us how to be generous instead of greedy. Guide us into generosity, selflessness, and into the joy of giving. Amen

ATTACKING

Attack: to set upon in a forceful, violent, hostile, or aggressive way, with or without a weapon.

Differences, disagreements, arguments, and yes even fights are inevitable in long-term close relationships. Marriage is no exception. Two people brought up in different circumstances, with different religious backgrounds, with different kinds of schooling, with different interests, with different dreams and aspirations, with different personalities, with different likes and dislikes are going to butt heads at times. That is understandable and normal. Discussions over disagreements can be healthy, depending on the manner in which those disagreements are handled.

Attacking the other person in forceful aggressive hostile ways is not a healthy way to fight. The first rule of fair fighting is that there be no attacking, either physically or verbally. Name-calling, critical put-downs, and digging up dirt from the past will not resolve the problem about which there is a disagreement. Attacking makes the other person defensive, and he or she is likely to respond with an attack of his or her own. Back and forth the attacks will escalate as tempers get hotter, and the need to defend oneself gets stronger. The outcome commonly is that with a finger gesture and a command to go do something to oneself, the male goes off in a huff. Or the outcome often is that she goes off in tears. Nothing has been resolved. The relationship has been weakened. Feelings of tenderness and affection are not part of the scenario. Silence between the two follows, sometimes for hours, sometimes for days, sometimes for weeks.

Fair fighting makes no allowance for attacks. Attacking is the kind of action that gets a football player thrown out of the game. Fair fighting includes stating openly what you think, what you feel, and what you want. "I think that we've been spending more money than we can afford, and I feel scared about that because I don't like to be in debt, and I'd like us to go over our budget to see where we can cut back." No attack. No accusation. No name-calling. No blaming.

"I think that we've become so busy with work, church, the kids, and helping with our parents that we've not had enough time just for the two of us. I'm feeling sad about that, and I'd like us to talk about how you and I can find some time for us to be together in ways that will strengthen our relationship." No attack. No accusation. No name-calling. No blaming.

Problems, disagreements, differences, and arguments are certain to happen in a marriage. The first step in making sure that the way we deal with them is to agree on forbidding attacks. Instead, use the formula "I think, I feel, I want" to deal with disagreements and differences. And never use the words "never" as in "you never," as in "you always . . ." or the word "always" as in "you always. . ."

For discussion: Why does attacking not work? Practice the fair fighting method of "I think, I feel, I want" right now.

Prayer: When we get mad at each other, remind us not to attack. Amen

AUDACITY

Audacity: impertinence; imprudence

Impertinent: inappropriate; disrespectful; insolent

Imprudence: rash; disrespectful; without thought of consequences; not sensible; not exercising sound judgment

To be audacious is be make rash, non-sensible, unsound decisions and judgments. Although President Barack Obama uses the word "audacity" in a positive way for the title of his book, The Audacity of Hope, audacity is not a healthy, positive characteristic to have in a marriage. Audacity in one or both of the marriage partners is destructive and counter-productive. An audacious person is impertinent, imprudent, inappropriate, disrespectful, insolent, rash, and, without considering possible consequences, makes decisions that are not sensible and that do not show sound judgment.

The following examples could be descriptions of an audacious person:

- He spends the meager family income on non-essentials such as the newest in all the latest technological innovations, e.g. communication devices, the largest screen high definition TV, and the very best stereo system. All these items are purchased with a credit card.

- She shows no respect for his family's customs, ways of celebrating holidays, and their traditional religious observances.

119

- He inappropriately disregards long-established courtesies when attending social gatherings.

- She is a loud, boisterous, know-it-all who lets anyone and everyone know that she is always right, and everyone else is wrong, stupid, and intellectually inferior.

- He/she demonstrates arrogance and disrespect for others by not listening attentively, regularly interrupting the one who is speaking, and showing a total disregard for the other person's thoughts, interests, and life experiences.

In other words, audacity is seen in the person who is not prudent, I,e. is incapable of making sound judgments in practical matters; is not cautious in conduct; is not sensible, is rash; is indiscreet and egotistical. Needless to say, the audacious husband or wife is not an easy person to live with. Audacious people act as if they are God's gift to the world, and everyone else is a mere peasant or a poor excuse for a human being. The person characterized by audacity is insensitive, prideful, inconsiderate, and grossly self-centered. Such a person would have a hard time agreeing with the Scripture ". . . Do not think of yourself more highly than you ought . . ." (Romans 12:3) And the audacious person does not follow the counsel found in 1 Thessalonians 5:11, "Therefore encourage one another and build each other up . . ."

For discussion: How would you define "audacity?" How would you explain audacity to a child? Is either of us guilty of audacity? If one of us is audacious, how can the other one expect to be respected?

Prayer: Deliver us from audacity. If we are audacious, enable us to overcome it. And when my spouse sees audacity in me, help him/her to let me know, and help me to admit it and change it. Amen

If you are newly married . . .

or if you have been married for many years . . .

or if you are planning to be married . . .

or if you are considering marriage . . .

or if you would like to be married . . .

. . . this book is for you! Dave Ehline puts his pastoral knowledge and counseling experience in your hands with this easy to read book. Marriage is challenging, and marriage takes effort, time and commitment to bond two very different people into a single unit without destroying the unique individuality of either of the two. Marriage may not always be easy, but in this book you will find help and guidance for making your marriage satisfying, fulfilling, and gratifying. Reading and discussing this book can put you on the road to achieving an A+ marriage!

ABOUT THE AUTHOR

David Ehline received his B.A. degree from Gustavus Adolphus College, St. Peter, Minnesota, his Master of Divinity degree from Yale Divinity School, New Haven, Connecticut, and his Master of Social Work from the University of Nebraska, Lincoln. He is an ordained minister, having served congregations in California and Nebraska. He also enjoyed many years of special service as a clinical counselor at family services agencies, where he provided individual, couple, and family therapy. As an adjunct faculty member, he taught at the University of Nebraska, Omaha. His ministerial career culminated with years of service as a chaplain in a faith-based long-term care center, ministering to residents in skilled nursing, memory care, assisted living, and independent living. He and his wife Patricia are retired, and live in Castle Rock, CO.

CPSIA information can be obtained
at www.ICGtesting.com
Printed in the USA
FSOW04n0021250916
25337FS